Eclipsed Echoes of the Midnight Canopy

Unravel the Mysteries of the Night Sky and Celestial Wonders

Dana Ballard

Chapter 1: The Enchanting Realm of the Midnight Canopy

The Allure of the Night Sky

The night sky has long captivated the human imagination, serving as an expansive canvas painted with countless stars, planets, and celestial phenomena. This vast, dark expanse, dotted with shimmering lights, invites wonder and curiosity, drawing us into a world far removed from the humdrum of daily life. The allure of the night sky is a complex tapestry woven from scientific intrigue, cultural significance, and personal reflection, each thread contributing to its enduring mystique.

For millennia, people have looked up at the night sky, seeking answers and inspiration. Ancient civilizations meticulously observed the movements of stars and planets, crafting elaborate stories and myths to explain the celestial phenomena. These narratives became an integral part of their cultural heritage, demonstrating the profound impact the night sky has had on humanity's collective consciousness. From the Greeks and their tales of gods and heroes to the Chinese zodiac and its influence on personality traits, the sky has been a source of endless fascination.

The enchantment of the night sky goes beyond its visual splendor. It represents a gateway to the cosmos, a reminder of our place within the universe's grand design. The stars that twinkle above are not just points of light; they are distant suns, each with its own story of birth, life, and eventual demise. The constellations we recognize today are the same ones that guided ancient mariners across uncharted waters, offering a sense of direction and continuity amid the ever-changing seas.

Yet, the night sky's allure is not solely about distant stars and planets. It is also about the intimate connection we feel when gazing upwards. Standing beneath a velvet canopy sprinkled with stardust, we are reminded of the vastness of the universe and our own small place within it. This humbling perspective can evoke a sense of wonder and introspection, prompting us to ponder the mysteries of existence and our role in the cosmic order.

Light pollution, however, threatens this connection. In many urban areas, the brilliance of artificial lights drowns out the stars, obscuring our view of the night sky. The loss is more than aesthetic; it is a disconnection from the natural world, a diminishing of the awe that the night sky inspires. Efforts to mitigate light pollution, such as implementing dark sky preserves and encouraging responsible lighting practices, are crucial for preserving our celestial heritage.

Despite the challenges posed by modern life, stargazing remains an accessible and rewarding pursuit. With the right tools and a bit of patience, anyone can explore the wonders of the night sky. Telescopes, binoculars, and even the unaided eye can reveal a wealth of celestial treasures, from the glowing band of the Milky Way to the delicate dance of satellites and meteors. The night sky offers an ever-changing tableau, with new surprises waiting to be discovered each time we look up.

Stargazing is not just a solitary endeavor; it is an opportunity to connect with others. Amateur astronomers often gather to share their passion, exchanging knowledge and stories under the stars. These gatherings foster a sense of community and camaraderie, as enthusiasts from all walks of life come together to celebrate the wonders of the night sky. Through shared experiences, we deepen our appreciation for the cosmos and the bonds that unite us as inhabitants of this planet.

The allure of the night sky is also a call to exploration. The mysteries that lie beyond our atmosphere beckon us to venture into the unknown, to seek out new worlds and phenomena. This spirit of discovery has driven scientific advancements and technological innovations, propelling humanity to the moon and beyond. The night sky serves as both a source of inspiration and a reminder of the vast potential that lies within us to explore, learn, and grow.

In the quiet moments spent beneath the stars, we find solace and perspective. The night sky invites us to pause, to breathe, and to reflect on the beauty and complexity of the universe. It rekindles a sense of awe and curiosity, reminding us that there is always more to explore and understand. As we gaze upward, we are reminded that we are part of something much larger than ourselves, connected to a cosmic tapestry that spans time and space.

Historical Perspectives on Celestial Observations

Throughout history, celestial observations have played a pivotal role in shaping human understanding of the universe. From ancient civilizations to the modern era, the study of the night sky has influenced science, religion, and culture in profound ways. These historical perspectives provide a fascinating glimpse into how humanity has sought to comprehend the cosmos and its own place within it.

In ancient Mesopotamia, the Babylonians were among the first to systematically observe the heavens, meticulously recording the movements of celestial bodies. They developed one of the earliest known zodiac systems, using it to predict astronomical events and guide agricultural practices. The Babylonians' observations laid the groundwork for future astronomical studies, highlighting the practical importance of celestial phenomena in daily life.

The Egyptians, too, were keen observers of the night sky. Their understanding of celestial movements was deeply intertwined with their religious beliefs and architectural achievements. The alignment of the pyramids with certain stars, particularly the North Star, demonstrates their sophisticated knowledge of astronomy. The annual flooding of the Nile River was predicted based on the heliacal rising of the star Sirius, underscoring the Egyptians' reliance on celestial events for agricultural planning.

In ancient Greece, astronomy was both a scientific and philosophical pursuit. Greek scholars like Pythagoras and Ptolemy made significant contributions to the understanding of celestial mechanics. Pythagoras proposed the idea of a spherical Earth, while Ptolemy's geocentric model of the universe, described in the Almagest, dominated Western thought for over a millennium. These early theories, though later revised, were instrumental in advancing the study of the cosmos.

The Chinese also made remarkable strides in celestial observations. Their meticulous records of comets, eclipses, and supernovae date back to as early as the 4th century BCE. The Chinese developed a lunar calendar based on their observations, which played a crucial role in agriculture and governance. Their systematic approach to recording celestial events contributed to a rich tradition of astronomical scholarship that influenced neighboring cultures.

The Islamic Golden Age marked a period of significant advancements in astronomy. Muslim astronomers built upon the foundations laid by their Greek and Indian predecessors, making notable contributions to celestial navigation and instrumentation. Figures like Al-Battani and Al-Sufi refined existing models of planetary motion and compiled detailed star catalogs. These scholars also established observatories, fostering a culture of scientific inquiry and collaboration.

The Renaissance era witnessed a resurgence of interest in celestial observations, fueled by the invention of the telescope. Galileo Galilei's use of this revolutionary instrument unveiled previously unseen details of the night sky, such as the moons of Jupiter and the phases of Venus. His observations provided crucial evidence for the heliocentric model proposed by Nicolaus Copernicus, challenging the long-held geocentric view and transforming the field of astronomy.

In the 17th century, Johannes Kepler and Isaac Newton further revolutionized celestial mechanics with their groundbreaking work. Kepler's laws of planetary motion described the elliptical orbits of planets, while Newton's law of universal gravitation provided a unifying framework for understanding the forces governing celestial bodies. These discoveries laid the foundation for modern astrophysics, enabling more accurate predictions of astronomical phenomena.

The 19th and 20th centuries brought about unprecedented advancements in celestial observations. The development of photography and spectroscopy allowed astronomers to study the composition and behavior of stars in greater detail. Observatories equipped with powerful telescopes, such as the Mount Wilson Observatory, expanded our view of the universe, revealing distant galaxies and nebulae. These technological innovations opened new frontiers in the exploration of the cosmos.

The space age marked a new chapter in celestial observations, as humanity ventured beyond Earth's atmosphere. The launch of space telescopes, such as the Hubble Space Telescope, provided unprecedented views of the universe, capturing breathtaking images of distant galaxies, nebulae, and other celestial wonders. Space missions to other planets and moons further enriched our understanding of the solar system and its origins.

Today, celestial observations continue to captivate and inspire. Modern astronomers utilize cutting-edge technology and international collaborations to probe the mysteries of the universe, from the search for exoplanets to the study of dark matter and energy. The legacy of historical perspectives on celestial observations serves as a testament to humanity's enduring curiosity and quest for knowledge.

The Impact of Light Pollution

The splendor of the night sky has inspired poets, scientists, and dreamers for countless generations. However, in our modern world, the brilliance of celestial wonders is increasingly obscured by an artificial glow that poses a threat not only to our ability to appreciate the stars but also to the environment and our well-being. Light pollution, a byproduct of urbanization and technological advancement, has far-reaching consequences that extend beyond the mere loss of starlight.

Light pollution primarily manifests in three forms: skyglow, glare, and light trespass. Skyglow is the brightening of the night sky over populated areas, caused by artificial lights scattering in the atmosphere. This phenomenon diminishes the visibility of stars and other celestial objects, reducing the majesty of the night sky to a faint glimmer. Glare refers to excessive brightness that causes visual discomfort, often emanating from poorly designed lighting fixtures. Light trespass occurs when unwanted artificial light spills into areas where it is neither needed nor desired, disrupting the natural dark environment.

The environmental impact of light pollution is profound. Nocturnal animals, whose survival depends on the cover of darkness, are particularly vulnerable. Artificial lighting disrupts their natural behaviors, such as mating, foraging, and migration. Sea turtles, for instance, rely on the moon's reflection on the ocean to guide hatchlings to the sea. Artificial lights can disorient these hatchlings, leading them away from safety and towards perilous urban environments. Similarly, migratory birds, which navigate using the stars, can become confused by city lights, resulting in fatal collisions with buildings.

Beyond its ecological effects, light pollution also has implications for human health. The disruption of natural light cycles interferes with our circadian rhythms, the internal clocks governing our sleep-wake patterns. Exposure to artificial light at night can suppress the production of melatonin, a hormone that regulates sleep. This disruption can lead to sleep disorders, increased stress, and a heightened risk of chronic health issues such as obesity and cardiovascular disease. Furthermore, studies suggest that excessive nighttime lighting may be linked to an increased risk of certain cancers.

The cultural and scientific ramifications of light pollution are equally significant. Throughout history, the night sky has served as a canvas for storytelling, a source of inspiration, and a tool for navigation. The loss of starry nights deprives us of this shared heritage, diminishing our connection to the cosmos. For astronomers, both amateur and professional, light pollution creates substantial challenges. Observatories situated near urban areas face reduced visibility, making it difficult to conduct research and observe celestial phenomena. This hampers our ability to explore and understand the universe, stifling scientific advancement.

Mitigating the impact of light pollution requires a multifaceted approach. One of the most effective strategies is the implementation of responsible lighting practices. This involves using lighting fixtures that minimize glare and direct light only where it is needed. Shielded fixtures, for example, prevent light from spilling upwards into the sky, reducing skyglow. Additionally, utilizing energy-efficient bulbs with lower wattage and warmer color temperatures can decrease overall light emissions.

Public awareness and education are crucial in the fight against light pollution. Encouraging communities to recognize the benefits of preserving dark skies can lead to collective action and policy changes. Initiatives such as International Dark Sky Week and the establishment of dark sky preserves raise awareness about the importance of protecting our nocturnal environment. These efforts not only promote ecological and scientific benefits but also enhance the quality of life for residents by creating more peaceful and visually appealing surroundings.

Regulatory measures also play a vital role in addressing light pollution. Municipalities can implement ordinances that enforce lighting standards, ensuring that outdoor lighting is both efficient and considerate of the night environment. These regulations can include requirements for motion sensors, timers, and curfews to reduce unnecessary lighting during nighttime hours. By prioritizing the conservation of dark skies, local governments can set a precedent for sustainable urban planning that respects both human and ecological needs.

Technological advancements continue to offer innovative solutions to combat light pollution. Smart lighting systems, which adjust brightness and color based on time of day and environmental conditions, provide a promising way to balance illumination with conservation. These systems utilize sensors and automation to optimize lighting, reducing waste and minimizing impact on the night sky. As technology evolves, the integration of such systems into urban infrastructure has the potential to transform our relationship with artificial light.

The journey to reclaim the night sky is not solely the responsibility of policymakers and scientists; individuals also have a role to play. Simple actions, such as turning off unnecessary lights, utilizing blackout curtains, and advocating for community-based initiatives, contribute to the collective effort to reduce light pollution. By fostering a sense of stewardship and appreciation for the night sky, we can work towards a future where the stars are once again a prominent feature of our nocturnal landscape.

Cultural Significance of the Night

Across the globe, the night sky has served as a profound source of inspiration, shaping the cultural tapestries of diverse societies. Beyond its celestial wonders, the nocturnal realm has been a canvas for myths, a guide for travelers, and a backdrop for sacred rituals. The cultural significance of the night is as vast and varied as the stars themselves, illuminating our shared human experience across time and space.

In ancient civilizations, the night sky was a dynamic theater where stories unfolded, connecting the heavens with the earthly realm. The constellations were not merely collections of stars; they were vibrant characters in epic tales. The Greeks populated the sky with gods and heroes, weaving narratives that explained natural phenomena and moral lessons. Orion, the great hunter, and Andromeda, the princess, were immortalized among the stars, their stories passed down through generations. These celestial myths provided a framework for understanding the world and humanity's place within it.

Beyond storytelling, the night sky held practical significance for early societies. For many, it served as a celestial calendar, guiding agricultural practices and marking the passage of time. The cycles of the moon were closely observed, dictating planting and harvesting schedules. The Maori of New Zealand, for instance, celebrated Matariki, the rising of the Pleiades star cluster, as the start of the new year and a time for planting. This celestial event was a crucial marker for the community, intertwining their cultural identity with the rhythms of the night sky.

Navigation by the stars was another vital aspect of the night's cultural significance. Mariners relied on the constellations to guide them across vast, uncharted oceans. The Polynesians, skilled navigators of the Pacific, used a sophisticated system of star paths to traverse the seas, reaching distant islands with remarkable precision. The North Star, Polaris, served as a steadfast beacon for travelers in the Northern Hemisphere, its unwavering position in the sky offering direction and stability. This reliance on celestial navigation underscores the deep connection between human exploration and the night sky.

The night also held spiritual and religious significance, serving as a bridge between the earthly and the divine. In many cultures, the movements of celestial bodies were seen as expressions of divine will or cosmic order. The ancient Egyptians believed that the sun god Ra journeyed through the underworld each night, emerging victorious at dawn. The Inca Empire revered Inti, the sun god, whose nightly disappearance and reappearance were celebrated with rituals and offerings. These beliefs underscored the night as a time of transformation and renewal, where the cycle of death and rebirth played out in the heavens.

In the realm of art and literature, the night has been a muse for countless creators. The interplay of light and shadow has inspired painters, poets, and musicians to capture the mystery and beauty of the nocturnal world. Vincent van Gogh's "Starry Night" is a vivid expression of the artist's fascination with the swirling heavens, while poets like John Keats and Robert Frost have woven the night into their verses, exploring themes of solitude, wonder, and introspection. The night's allure continues to inspire contemporary artists, who find in its depths a wellspring of creativity and reflection.

The cultural significance of the night extends to modern traditions and practices. In many societies, festivals and celebrations are held under the cover of darkness, where the night offers a sense of magic and wonder. Fireworks illuminate the sky during New Year's Eve and Independence Day celebrations, creating a spectacle that echoes the celestial displays above. The night markets of Asia come alive with vibrant colors and bustling energy, offering a sensory experience that captivates locals and tourists alike.

In recent years, the night sky has become a focal point for conservation efforts, as communities recognize the importance of preserving this cultural heritage. Dark sky initiatives aim to combat light pollution, ensuring that future generations can continue to experience the beauty and wonder of the stars. These efforts reflect a growing awareness of the night's role in our cultural identity and its value as a shared resource.

Tools for Stargazing

Gazing up at the night sky, one might feel a pang of longing to delve deeper into the mysteries that lie beyond our reach. The twinkling stars, the distant planets, and the ethereal glow of the moon beckon us to explore. While the naked eye can capture much of this celestial beauty, a variety of tools are available to enhance our stargazing experience and bring us closer to the wonders that adorn the night.

The most accessible tool for budding astronomers is a pair of binoculars. Often overlooked in favor of telescopes, binoculars are an excellent starting point for those eager to explore the night sky. Their wide field of view allows for easy location and observation of objects like the moon's craters, the moons of Jupiter, and star clusters such as the Pleiades. Binoculars are lightweight, portable, and relatively affordable, making them ideal for spontaneous stargazing sessions or for those who wish to explore the sky without a significant investment.

For those ready to take their celestial observations to the next level, a telescope opens up a realm of possibilities. Telescopes come in various types and sizes, each suited to different needs and preferences. Refractor telescopes, with their long tubes and lenses, are perfect for viewing planets and double stars. Reflector telescopes, which use mirrors, are better suited for deep-sky objects like galaxies and nebulae. Compound telescopes combine both lenses and mirrors, offering versatility for observing a wide range of celestial phenomena.

Selecting the right telescope depends on several factors, including budget, experience, and observing goals. Beginners may want to start with a smaller, more manageable telescope, while seasoned astronomers might invest in a larger, more advanced model. It's essential to consider the telescope's aperture, or the diameter of its main lens or mirror, as this determines its light-gathering capability and resolution. A larger aperture allows for clearer, more detailed views of faint objects.

In addition to the telescope itself, a stable mount is crucial for steady observations. An equatorial mount, which aligns with Earth's axis, allows for smooth tracking of celestial objects as they move across the sky. Alternatively, a simple altazimuth mount provides easy up-and-down, left-and-right movement, making it user-friendly for beginners. Motorized or computerized mounts offer added convenience by automatically tracking objects, allowing observers to focus on the view rather than adjusting the telescope manually.

The digital age has ushered in a new era of stargazing tools, with smartphone apps and software revolutionizing the way we explore the night sky. Apps like Stellarium, SkySafari, and Star Walk enable users to identify stars, planets, and constellations with the touch of a screen. By pointing a smartphone or tablet toward the sky, these apps overlay celestial maps, providing real-time information and guidance. They also offer features such as notifications for upcoming celestial events and customizable observing lists.

Astrophotography, the art of capturing images of celestial objects, is another exciting avenue for stargazers. With advances in camera technology, even amateur astronomers can produce stunning photographs of the night sky. A DSLR camera mounted on a tripod is a good starting point, allowing for long exposures that capture the intricate details of stars and constellations. More advanced setups may include specialized cameras attached to telescopes, enabling the capture of deep-sky objects like galaxies and nebulae.

For those interested in capturing the movement of the stars, time-lapse photography offers a captivating way to document the passage of time. By taking a series of images over several hours, photographers can create mesmerizing videos that reveal the rotation of the Earth and the dance of celestial bodies across the sky. This technique requires patience and careful planning but rewards with breathtaking visual narratives.

Joining a local astronomy club or group can provide invaluable support and resources for stargazers at any level. These communities often host star parties, where members gather to observe the night sky together, sharing equipment, expertise, and enthusiasm. Such gatherings offer opportunities to learn from experienced astronomers, try out different tools, and gain insights into the best observing practices.

For those seeking to deepen their knowledge, online forums and resources abound. Websites like Cloudy Nights and AstroBin offer platforms for astronomers to share their experiences, discuss equipment, and exchange tips on stargazing and astrophotography. Engaging with these communities can enhance one's understanding of the night sky and foster connections with fellow enthusiasts worldwide.

While tools and technology can significantly enhance the stargazing experience, it's essential to remember the value of patience and practice. The night sky is a vast and ever-changing canvas, requiring time and dedication to fully appreciate its wonders.

Familiarizing oneself with the constellations, learning to navigate the sky, and keeping a journal of observations can enrich the journey of exploration.

Chapter 2: Celestial Bodies and Their Mysteries

The Moon Phases and Phenomena

The moon, Earth's constant companion, has captivated humanity for millennia with its luminous beauty and rhythmic transformations. Its phases and phenomena have not only provided a basis for calendars but have also influenced cultural beliefs, scientific inquiry, and even human behavior. Understanding the moon's cycles and the extraordinary events associated with it can deepen our appreciation for this celestial body and its role in our lives.

The moon's phases arise from its orbit around Earth, which takes approximately 29.5 days to complete. This cycle, known as a lunation, is divided into eight distinct phases, each representing a different portion of the moon's sunlit side visible from Earth. The cycle begins with the new moon, a moment when the moon is positioned between Earth and the Sun, rendering it invisible to us. As it progresses to the waxing crescent, a sliver of light emerges, growing each night until it reaches the first quarter, where half of the moon's face is illuminated.

Following the first quarter, the moon enters the waxing gibbous phase, with more than half of its surface visible. This continues until the full moon, when the entire sunlit side faces Earth, bathing the night in its radiant glow. The cycle then moves into the waning phases, starting with the waning gibbous, as the illuminated portion gradually diminishes. The last quarter marks the return to a half-lit moon, leading to the waning crescent, and finally, back to the new moon.

Throughout history, the moon's phases have been essential in timekeeping. Many ancient cultures, such as the Babylonians and the Chinese, developed lunar calendars based on these cycles. Even today, some religious and cultural observances, like Ramadan in Islam and the Jewish Passover, are determined by the lunar calendar. The moon's phases provided a natural rhythm for agricultural societies, guiding planting and harvesting schedules in harmony with the changing night sky.

Beyond its phases, the moon presents a plethora of remarkable phenomena that continue to intrigue observers. One such event is the lunar eclipse, which occurs when Earth passes directly between the Sun and the moon, casting a shadow that can obscure the moon's light. Depending on the alignment, a lunar eclipse can be total, partial, or penumbral. During a total lunar eclipse, the moon often takes on a reddish hue, earning it the nickname "blood moon." This coloration is caused by Earth's atmosphere scattering sunlight, allowing only the longer, red wavelengths to reach the moon.

Another captivating phenomenon is the supermoon, which occurs when a full moon coincides with the moon's closest approach to Earth in its elliptical orbit, known as perigee. During a supermoon, the moon appears larger and brighter than usual, creating a stunning sight for skywatchers. In contrast, a micromoon occurs when the full moon is at its farthest point from Earth, or apogee, appearing slightly smaller and dimmer.

The moon also plays a significant role in tidal phenomena. Its gravitational pull, along with that of the Sun, influences Earth's oceans, creating the rhythmic rise and fall of tides. Spring tides, characterized by higher high tides and lower low tides, occur during new and full moons when the Sun, Earth, and moon are aligned, amplifying their gravitational effects. Neap tides, with less pronounced tidal differences, occur during the first and last quarters when the gravitational forces of the Sun and moon are perpendicular to each other.

Culturally, the moon has inspired a myriad of myths, legends, and traditions. Many ancient societies revered the moon as a deity or a divine entity. The Greeks worshipped Selene, the goddess of the moon, while the Romans honored Luna. For the Maya, the moon was associated with the goddess Ix Chel, a symbol of fertility and medicine. These beliefs underscore the moon's profound influence on human perception and spirituality.

The moon's phases and phenomena have also sparked scientific curiosity and exploration. The changing face of the moon led early astronomers to question its nature and composition. Galileo Galilei's telescopic observations in the 17th century revealed the moon's mountains and craters, challenging the prevailing notion of celestial perfection. These observations laid the groundwork for future lunar exploration, culminating in the Apollo missions that brought humans to the moon's surface.

In recent years, interest in the moon has been rekindled with plans for renewed exploration and potential habitation. The prospect of utilizing lunar resources, such as water ice in permanently shadowed craters, has sparked discussions about sustainable human presence on the moon. These endeavors not only aim to expand our scientific knowledge but also to inspire a new generation to look up and wonder at the moon's enduring mystery.

For stargazers and moon enthusiasts, observing the moon's phases and phenomena requires little more than a clear night and a curious mind. A pair of binoculars or a small telescope can enhance the experience, revealing intricate details such as the rugged surface of the moon and the play of light and shadow along the terminator, the line dividing the illuminated and dark sides. Keeping a lunar journal, recording observations, and noting changes over time can deepen one's connection to the moon and its cycles.

The Sun's Hidden Secrets

Beneath the blinding brilliance of the sun lies a world of hidden secrets and untold mysteries waiting to be unraveled. The sun, a colossal orb of incandescent gas, not only fuels life on Earth but also holds the key to understanding our solar system's dynamics. While its blazing surface might seem uniform and unchanging, it conceals a complex and ever-evolving interior that influences the cosmos in myriad ways.

At the core of the sun, nuclear fusion is the engine that powers this colossal star. Here, hydrogen atoms are fused into helium under immense pressure and temperature, releasing an astonishing amount of energy in the form of light and heat. This process, which has sustained the sun for billions of years, is the fundamental force that sustains life on Earth. Yet, the core itself remains shrouded in mystery, as its conditions are too extreme for direct observation. Scientists rely on indirect methods, such as helioseismology, to study the sun's internal structure. By analyzing the sun's oscillations—similar to seismic waves on Earth—researchers can infer details about its composition and dynamics.

Surrounding the core is the radiative zone, where energy produced in the core travels outward in the form of radiation. It can take thousands of years for this energy to pass through the dense radiative zone before reaching the convective zone. In this outer layer, energy transfer shifts from radiation to convection, with hot plasma rising to the surface, cooling, and then sinking back down in a continuous cycle. This dynamic motion creates the sun's magnetic field, a powerful force that shapes solar activity and influences space weather.

The sun's surface, known as the photosphere, is a tumultuous region where magnetic fields manifest as sunspots, cooler and darker patches that can be observed with the proper protective equipment. Sunspots are often precursors to solar flares and coronal mass ejections—massive bursts of solar material that can disrupt satellites, power grids, and communication systems on Earth. Understanding the mechanisms behind these phenomena is vital for predicting space weather and mitigating its impact on our technologically dependent society.

Just above the photosphere lies the chromosphere, a thin layer that emits a reddish glow observable during solar eclipses. This region is home to spicules, jets of solar material that shoot into the sun's outer atmosphere. Beyond the chromosphere is the corona, an expansive halo of hot plasma that extends millions of kilometers into space. The corona is paradoxically hotter than the sun's surface, a mystery that has puzzled scientists for decades. Recent observations from spacecraft like the Parker Solar Probe aim to shed light on this enigma, investigating how magnetic fields and wave heating might contribute to the corona's extreme temperatures.

The sun's magnetic field undergoes an 11-year cycle, during which its polarity reverses. This cycle is marked by periods of high and low solar activity, influencing the number of sunspots and solar flares. At the peak of solar activity, known as solar maximum, the sun is a hotbed of dynamic phenomena, with increased solar radiation impacting Earth's atmosphere and climate. Conversely, during solar minimum, the sun is relatively quiet, with fewer sunspots and flares. Tracking these cycles is crucial for understanding long-term climate patterns and preparing for potential disruptions to technology and infrastructure.

One of the sun's most profound influences on Earth is the aurora, a dazzling display of lights in polar regions caused by solar particles interacting with Earth's magnetic field. These particles, carried by the solar wind, excite atoms in the atmosphere, resulting in ethereal curtains of green, red, and purple light. While the aurora is a breathtaking spectacle, it also serves as a reminder of the sun's capacity to affect our planet directly.

The sun's secrets extend beyond its immediate vicinity, affecting the entire solar system. The heliosphere, a vast bubble of solar wind that envelops the solar system, acts as a shield against cosmic rays from interstellar space. Understanding the heliosphere's boundaries and behavior is essential for space exploration and the safety of astronauts venturing beyond Earth's protective magnetic field.

The quest to unveil the sun's hidden secrets has driven scientific innovation and exploration. From ancient astronomers who tracked its movements to modern-day spacecraft that venture close to its fiery surface, humanity's fascination with the sun has fueled advancements in technology and our understanding of the universe. Missions like the Solar Dynamics Observatory and the upcoming European Space Agency's Solar Orbiter continue to provide invaluable insights into the sun's behavior and its impact on the solar system.

Despite our progress, many of the sun's mysteries remain unsolved. The intricate interplay of magnetic fields, plasma, and energy within the sun is a complex puzzle that scientists are still piecing together. As our tools and techniques evolve, so too does our ability to probe deeper into the sun's secrets, bringing us closer to unlocking the profound mysteries that lie at the heart of our solar system's life-giving star.

Planets and Their Orbits

In the vast expanse of our solar system, planets move in a graceful ballet, each following a unique path around the sun. These celestial wanderers, with their distinct characteristics and orbits, offer a window into the dynamics of our cosmic neighborhood and the forces that govern it. Understanding the intricacies of planetary orbits not only enriches our knowledge of the solar system but also sheds light on the broader mechanics of the universe.

The concept of planetary orbits has fascinated humans for centuries, dating back to ancient astronomers who meticulously observed the night sky. They noted that while most stars remained fixed relative to one another, certain bright objects—planets—appeared to wander, moving against the backdrop of the constellations. This movement was puzzling, yet it laid the groundwork for one of the most significant breakthroughs in astronomy: the heliocentric model.

In the 16th century, Nicolaus Copernicus proposed a revolutionary idea: the sun, not the Earth, was the center of the solar system. This heliocentric model explained the apparent retrograde motion of planets as Earth overtakes or is overtaken by them in their orbits. The work of Johannes Kepler further refined this model. Kepler formulated three laws of planetary motion, which describe the elliptical orbits of planets and their varying speeds as they move around the sun.

Kepler's first law, the Law of Ellipses, states that planets orbit the sun in elliptical paths, with the sun at one focus of the ellipse. This means that the distance between a planet and the sun changes throughout its orbit, affecting the planet's speed and position in the sky. Kepler's second law, the Law of Equal Areas, asserts that a line segment joining a planet and the sun sweeps out equal areas during equal intervals of time. This implies that planets move faster when closer to the sun and slower when farther away.

Kepler's third law, the Law of Harmonies, reveals a relationship between the periods of planets' orbits and their average distances from the sun. Specifically, the square of a planet's orbital period is proportional to the cube of its semi-major axis—the longest diameter of its elliptical orbit. This law highlights the harmony and predictability inherent in the solar system's structure.

The study of planetary orbits has been greatly enhanced by advancements in technology and observation. With the advent of telescopes and space probes, astronomers have been able to observe planets with unprecedented detail, confirming and expanding upon Kepler's laws. These observations have revealed the diversity of planetary systems, with each planet exhibiting unique characteristics and behaviors.

Mercury, the innermost planet, possesses the most eccentric orbit of all the planets in our solar system.

Its proximity to the sun and rapid orbital speed contribute to extreme temperature variations on its surface. Venus, often referred to as Earth's twin due to its similar size and composition, follows a nearly circular orbit, resulting in a stable climate despite its thick, greenhouse gas-laden atmosphere.

Earth's orbit is nearly circular, with minimal eccentricity, providing a relatively stable climate that supports life. The tilt of Earth's axis, combined with its orbit, gives rise to the changing seasons, a phenomenon not shared by all planets. Mars, with its reddish hue and intriguing surface features, follows an elliptical orbit that brings it closer to Earth at certain times, making it a prime target for exploration.

The gas giants—Jupiter, Saturn, Uranus, and Neptune—occupy the outer reaches of the solar system, each with its own set of moons and rings. Jupiter, the largest planet, boasts a strong gravitational pull that influences the orbits of nearby objects, including asteroids and comets. Its orbit, while more distant from the sun, plays a crucial role in shaping the architecture of the solar system.

Saturn's orbit, adorned with its iconic rings, provides a stunning view through telescopes. The planet's numerous moons, each with its own orbit, create a complex system of interactions that captivate astronomers. Uranus and Neptune, the ice giants, follow distant orbits that take them far from the sun's warmth, resulting in frigid temperatures and unique atmospheric conditions.

Beyond the planets, countless other celestial bodies traverse the solar system, each with its own path. Asteroids and comets, remnants of the solar system's formation, follow diverse orbits that can bring them close to the sun or fling them into the outer reaches of the solar system. The Kuiper Belt and Oort Cloud, regions teeming with icy bodies, represent the frontier of our solar neighborhood, with orbits that extend far beyond Neptune.

The study of planetary orbits has profound implications for understanding the origins and evolution of the solar system. By analyzing the orbits of planets and other celestial bodies, scientists can infer the processes that shaped our cosmic neighborhood. These insights inform our search for exoplanets—planets orbiting other stars—which may harbor conditions suitable for life.

In recent years, the discovery of exoplanets has revolutionized our understanding of planetary systems. Many of these distant worlds exhibit orbits vastly different from those in our solar system, challenging existing theories and prompting new questions about the diversity and complexity of planetary formation. The study of exoplanetary orbits offers a glimpse into the myriad ways in which planets can evolve and interact with their host stars.

Stars Birth, Life, and Death

Amidst the vast tapestry of the universe, stars emerge as brilliant beacons, illuminating the night sky with their radiant light. These celestial bodies, seemingly eternal and unchanging, are in fact dynamic entities with life cycles that span millions to billions of years. From their tumultuous births to their glorious deaths, stars undergo transformative processes that shape the cosmos and influence the very fabric of existence.

The journey of a star begins within the dark, cold reaches of a molecular cloud, also known as a stellar nursery. These immense regions of gas and dust are scattered throughout galaxies, providing the raw materials necessary for star formation. Within these clouds, gravitational forces draw matter together, causing regions to collapse and form dense cores. As these cores contract, their temperatures and pressures rise, igniting the process that will lead to the birth of a star.

Once a core reaches a critical temperature, nuclear fusion ignites, marking the transition from a protostar to a main-sequence star. In this phase, hydrogen atoms fuse into helium in the star's core, releasing energy that counterbalances gravitational collapse. The star enters a period of stability, its outward radiation pressure balancing the inward pull of gravity. The length of a star's main-sequence phase depends on its mass; more massive stars burn through their fuel quickly, while smaller stars can remain in this stage for billions of years.

The mass of a star is the determining factor in its evolutionary path. Low-mass stars, like our sun, have a gentler life cycle compared to their more massive counterparts. As a low-mass star exhausts its hydrogen fuel, it expands into a red giant, shedding its outer layers and leaving behind a hot core. This core becomes a white dwarf, a dense, dimly glowing remnant that will slowly cool over time.

In contrast, high-mass stars lead more tumultuous lives. As they burn through their hydrogen, they begin fusing heavier elements in a series of increasingly violent stages. This process culminates in a dramatic supernova explosion, a cataclysmic event that disperses the star's outer layers into the cosmos, enriching it with elements that will form new stars, planets, and even life. The core that remains may collapse into a neutron star or, if massive enough, a black hole—a region of space where gravity is so intense that not even light can escape.

The remnants of supernovae, known as supernova remnants, are among the most spectacular phenomena in the universe. These expanding shells of gas and dust glow brightly in various wavelengths, providing astronomers with insights into the processes of star formation and the synthesis of elements. It is within these remnants that the building blocks of life are forged, as the fusion processes in stars create elements like carbon, nitrogen, and oxygen, which are essential for life as we know it.

The death of a star is not an end but a new beginning. The material expelled during a star's demise becomes part of the interstellar medium, contributing to the formation of new stars and planetary systems. This cycle of birth, life, and death is a testament to the interconnectedness of the cosmos, where each star plays a role in the grand cosmic narrative.

Throughout history, stars have been objects of fascination and wonder. Ancient civilizations looked to the stars for guidance, navigation, and inspiration, weaving them into myths and legends that endure to this day. Modern astronomy has expanded our understanding of stars, revealing their complex life cycles and the profound impact they have on the universe.

Observing stars requires patience and a keen eye. For amateur astronomers, understanding the various stages of a star's life can enhance the stargazing experience. The night sky offers a glimpse into the past, as the light from distant stars takes thousands or even millions of years to reach us. By studying the different colors and brightness of stars, one can infer their age, composition, and place in their life cycle.

Red giants, with their distinctive hue, mark the later stages of a star's life, while blue supergiants are young, massive stars that burn brightly but have short lifespans. Binary star systems, where two stars orbit each other, can provide additional insights into stellar evolution, as their interactions can lead to unique phenomena like novae and x-ray binaries.

As we gaze upon the stars, we are reminded of the ephemeral nature of existence and the cycles of creation and destruction that govern the universe. These celestial beacons not only light up the night sky but also illuminate the path of scientific discovery, guiding us toward a deeper understanding of the cosmos and our place within it.

The Intrigue of Black Holes

Among the most enigmatic and captivating phenomena in the cosmos are black holes—regions of space where gravity is so intense that nothing, not even light, can escape. These cosmic enigmas challenge our understanding of physics and continue to intrigue scientists and enthusiasts alike. Their existence raises profound questions about the nature of space, time, and the universe itself, inviting us to explore their mysteries with curiosity and wonder.

Black holes are born from the remnants of massive stars that have undergone a supernova explosion. When such a star exhausts its nuclear fuel, its core collapses under the force of gravity, compressing its mass into an incredibly small volume. If the core's mass exceeds a critical threshold—approximately three times that of our sun—it collapses into a singularity, a point of infinite density where conventional physics breaks down. Surrounding this singularity is the event horizon, the boundary beyond which nothing can return once crossed.

The concept of black holes, while seemingly modern, has roots tracing back to the 18th century. The English clergyman and physicist John Michell first proposed the idea of "dark stars" with gravitational pull so strong that light could not escape. However, it wasn't until Albert Einstein's theory of general relativity in the early 20th century that the mathematical framework for black holes was established. Einstein's equations suggested that massive objects warp the fabric of space-time, creating the conditions necessary for black holes to exist.

Despite their invisibility, black holes reveal themselves through their interactions with surrounding matter. As material spirals into a black hole, it forms an accretion disk, heating up and emitting intense radiation that can be detected by telescopes. This radiation provides a means to study black holes indirectly, offering clues about their properties and behavior. The first black hole candidate, Cygnus X-1, was discovered in 1964 as a bright x-ray source in the constellation Cygnus, and subsequent observations have confirmed the existence of many more.

Black holes come in various sizes, from stellar-mass black holes formed by collapsing stars to supermassive black holes residing at the centers of galaxies. These supermassive black holes, with masses ranging from millions to billions of solar masses, play a crucial role in the dynamics of galaxies and the formation of cosmic structures. The discovery of a supermassive black hole at the center of our Milky Way, known as Sagittarius A*, has provided valuable insights into the relationship between black holes and their host galaxies.

The study of black holes has led to groundbreaking advancements in theoretical physics. One of the most intriguing aspects is Hawking radiation, a theoretical prediction by physicist Stephen Hawking. According to quantum mechanics, black holes are not entirely black; they can emit radiation due to quantum fluctuations near the event horizon. This phenomenon suggests that black holes can slowly lose mass and eventually evaporate over time, challenging the notion of information loss and posing questions about the fate of matter consumed by black holes.

The exploration of black holes also ventures into the realm of science fiction, sparking the imagination with possibilities of wormholes and time travel. While these concepts remain speculative, they highlight the allure of black holes as natural laboratories for testing the limits of our understanding of the universe. The idea of traversing a black hole to access other regions of space-time captivates the imagination, inspiring countless stories and theories.

Recent advancements in technology have allowed scientists to capture images of black holes for the first time. In 2019, the Event Horizon Telescope collaboration unveiled the first-ever image of a black hole's event horizon in the galaxy M87, providing direct visual evidence of their existence. This achievement marked a monumental step in the study of black holes, confirming theoretical predictions and opening new avenues for exploration.

Black holes also play a role in the universe's grand narrative, influencing the evolution of galaxies and the distribution of matter. Their immense gravitational pull can trigger the formation of stars and influence the motion of nearby celestial objects. Supermassive black holes, in particular, are thought to regulate the growth of galaxies through feedback mechanisms, where energy released by accretion processes can drive powerful jets of particles and influence star formation.

For those fascinated by the mysteries of the cosmos, black holes offer a captivating subject for study and observation. Amateurs and professionals alike can engage with the wonders of black holes through astrophotography, data analysis, and theoretical research. The allure of these cosmic phenomena lies not only in their scientific significance but also in their ability to inspire awe and curiosity about the universe's hidden depths.

Chapter 3: Cosmic Events That Captivate

Solar and Lunar Eclipses

The mesmerizing dance of celestial bodies occasionally aligns in such a way that the sun, moon, and Earth form a straight line, resulting in the captivating phenomena of solar and lunar eclipses. These cosmic events have fascinated humanity for millennia, inspiring awe, wonder, and sometimes fear. Understanding the mechanics behind eclipses not only demystifies these occurrences but also enhances our appreciation of the intricate choreography of the solar system.

Solar eclipses occur when the moon passes directly between the Earth and the sun, casting a shadow on our planet. This can only happen during a new moon, when the moon's illuminated side is facing away from Earth. Depending on the alignment, a solar eclipse can be total, partial, or annular. In a total solar eclipse, the moon completely covers the sun's disk, plunging a narrow path on Earth into temporary darkness. Observers within this path experience a dramatic shift from day to night, witnessing the sun's corona—a halo of plasma that is usually obscured by the sun's brightness.

A partial solar eclipse, on the other hand, occurs when only a portion of the sun is obscured by the moon, creating a crescent shape. In an annular solar eclipse, the moon is too far from Earth to completely cover the sun, resulting in a ring of sunlight encircling the moon's silhouette, often referred to as the "ring of fire." The type of solar eclipse experienced depends on the distance between the Earth, moon, and sun, as well as the observer's location.

Lunar eclipses, by contrast, occur when the Earth positions itself between the sun and the moon, casting its shadow upon the moon. This event can only take place during a full moon, when the moon is on the opposite side of Earth from the sun. Lunar eclipses can be total, partial, or penumbral. In a total lunar eclipse, the entire moon enters Earth's umbra—the central, darkest part of its shadow—resulting in a striking transformation. The moon takes on a reddish hue, often called a "blood moon," due to Earth's atmosphere scattering sunlight and allowing only the longer, red wavelengths to reach the moon.

A partial lunar eclipse occurs when only a part of the moon enters the umbra, while a penumbral lunar eclipse happens when the moon passes through Earth's penumbra, the lighter outer shadow. Penumbral eclipses are subtle and can be difficult to observe, as the moon's brightness is only slightly diminished.

The geometry of eclipses is remarkable, given the relative sizes and distances of the sun, moon, and Earth. The sun is about 400 times larger than the moon but also approximately 400 times farther away, allowing the moon to occasionally cover the sun's disk from our perspective. This precise alignment is what makes total solar eclipses possible, though they are rare and occur only in specific regions along the Earth's surface.

Eclipses have played significant roles in human history and culture. Ancient civilizations often regarded them as omens, attributing them to the actions of gods or supernatural forces. Some cultures developed elaborate rituals to ward off perceived dangers associated with eclipses. In contrast, others observed and recorded these events, contributing to our understanding of celestial mechanics.

The ability to predict eclipses with accuracy is a testament to our progress in astronomy and mathematics. Ancient astronomers, such as the Babylonians and Greeks, made significant strides in eclipse prediction by identifying patterns in their occurrence. The Saros cycle, a period of approximately 18 years, 11 days, and 8 hours, is one such pattern that has been used to forecast eclipses for centuries. This cycle arises from the alignment of the sun, Earth, and moon, repeating after this interval due to their orbital periods.

For modern observers, eclipses offer unique opportunities for scientific study and public engagement. Solar eclipses, in particular, provide a rare chance to study the sun's corona, which is crucial for understanding solar activity and its impact on space weather. During a total solar eclipse, astronomers can observe the corona's structure, temperature, and magnetic fields, gaining insights into solar flares and coronal mass ejections that can affect Earth's technology and climate.

Lunar eclipses, while not as visually dramatic as total solar eclipses, are accessible to a wider audience, as they can be observed from anywhere on the night side of Earth. They offer a chance to study the Earth's atmosphere, as the color and intensity of the moon's reddish hue can provide information about atmospheric composition and conditions.

For those interested in observing an eclipse, preparation is key. Solar eclipses require special precautions, as looking directly at the sun can cause serious eye damage. Solar viewing glasses, solar filters for telescopes, or pinhole projectors can safely facilitate the experience. Lunar eclipses, being less hazardous, can be enjoyed with the naked eye, binoculars, or a telescope.

Eclipses also inspire artistic and cultural expressions, capturing the imagination and creativity of people across the globe. From ancient myths to modern literature and art, these celestial events have served as powerful symbols of transformation, renewal, and the passage of time.

In the realm of education, eclipses offer opportunities to engage learners of all ages with hands-on activities and interdisciplinary lessons. By exploring the science, history, and cultural significance of eclipses, educators can foster curiosity and a deeper understanding of our place in the universe.

Meteor Showers Nature's Fireworks

Streaking across the night sky like celestial fireworks, meteor showers captivate observers with their fleeting brilliance and ethereal beauty. These dazzling displays, known as nature's fireworks, occur when

Earth passes through the debris left behind by comets or asteroids. As these tiny particles—called meteoroids—enter Earth's atmosphere at high speeds, they burn up, producing the bright streaks of light we call meteors. Understanding the origins, mechanics, and viewing opportunities of meteor showers can enhance the experience for beginners and seasoned stargazers alike.

The origin of meteor showers lies in the trails of dust and debris shed by comets as they travel through the solar system. Comets, composed of ice, dust, and rocky material, develop tails of gas and dust when they approach the sun. As the sun's heat causes the comet's ice to vaporize, it releases particles along its orbit. When Earth intersects these trails, the resulting meteor showers occur annually, with the most famous being associated with specific comets.

One of the most well-known meteor showers is the Perseids, which peaks in mid-August. The Perseids are linked to the comet Swift-Tuttle, and their radiant—the point in the sky from which the meteors appear to originate—lies in the constellation Perseus. The Perseids are renowned for their high meteor count and bright meteors, making them a favorite among observers.

Another notable shower is the Leonids, which occur in November and are associated with the comet Tempel-Tuttle. The Leonids are known for producing meteor storms—intense outbursts with hundreds or even thousands of meteors per hour—approximately every 33 years when Earth passes through a particularly dense part of the comet's debris trail.

The Geminids, which peak in December, are unique as they originate from an asteroid rather than a comet. The asteroid 3200 Phaethon is responsible for this shower, which is known for its bright, slow-moving meteors. The Geminids' radiant is located in the constellation Gemini, and the shower is considered one of the most reliable and spectacular of the year.

Observing meteor showers requires minimal equipment, making them accessible to anyone with a clear view of the night sky. The best time to watch is during the shower's peak, typically occurring in the pre-dawn hours when the sky is darkest and the radiant is highest. For an optimal experience, find a location with minimal light pollution, such as a rural area or a designated dark sky park. Lie back on a blanket or reclining chair to take in as much of the sky as possible, and allow your eyes to adjust to the darkness for at least 20 minutes.

While meteor showers are predictable, the number of meteors visible can vary depending on several factors, including the brightness of the moon and weather conditions. A moonless night provides ideal viewing conditions, as the absence of lunar light enhances the visibility of meteors. Patience is key when observing meteor showers, as the frequency and brightness of meteors can fluctuate throughout the night.

Meteor showers not only provide a visual spectacle but also offer scientific insights into the composition and behavior of comets and asteroids. By studying the light emitted by meteors, scientists can determine the chemical makeup of the particles, shedding light on the conditions present in the early solar system.

Additionally, meteor showers can provide clues about the dynamics of cometary orbits and how they evolve over time.

For those interested in capturing meteor showers through photography, a few basic techniques can enhance the results. A camera with manual settings, a wide-angle lens, and a sturdy tripod are essential for long-exposure shots. Set the camera to a high ISO, use a shutter speed of 20 to 30 seconds, and experiment with different apertures to achieve the best results. Aim the camera toward the radiant, but be sure to include a portion of the surrounding sky to capture meteors that appear away from the radiant.

Meteor showers also offer opportunities for educational and community engagement. Hosting a meteor shower viewing event can bring together people of all ages to share in the wonder of the night sky. Providing informative talks about the origins and significance of meteor showers can enrich the experience and foster a deeper appreciation for astronomy.

In addition to their visual appeal, meteor showers have a rich cultural and historical significance. Many ancient cultures viewed meteors as omens or messages from the gods, attributing them to supernatural forces. Today, meteor showers continue to inspire art, literature, and folklore, serving as symbols of beauty and transformation.

As we gaze upon the fleeting brilliance of meteor showers, we are reminded of the dynamic and ever-changing nature of the cosmos. These celestial displays are a testament to the interconnectedness of celestial bodies and the ongoing dance of the solar system. They invite us to pause and reflect on the vastness of the universe and our place within it, offering moments of wonder and introspection.

The Dance of the Northern Lights

The ethereal display of the aurora borealis, or northern lights, paints the night sky with vibrant hues of green, pink, and violet, captivating those fortunate enough to witness its celestial dance. This natural light show, visible in high-latitude regions near the Arctic Circle, is both a scientific marvel and a source of cultural enrichment, inspiring awe and wonder across generations. Understanding the origins, mechanics, and viewing opportunities of the northern lights can enhance the appreciation of this mesmerizing phenomenon.

The northern lights are a result of charged particles from the sun interacting with Earth's magnetic field and atmosphere. The sun continuously emits a stream of charged particles known as the solar wind. When these particles reach Earth, they are drawn toward the poles by the planet's magnetic field. As the charged particles collide with gases in the atmosphere, primarily oxygen and nitrogen, they excite the gas molecules, causing them to emit light. This process creates the vibrant colors of the aurora, with green being the most common, resulting from oxygen molecules, while nitrogen can produce subtle reds and purples.

The aurora borealis is typically visible in regions around the Arctic Circle, including parts of Canada, Alaska, Scandinavia, and Russia. However, during periods of intense solar activity, the aurora can be seen at lower latitudes, extending its reach to more southerly locations. These periods of heightened activity, known as geomagnetic storms, occur when the sun releases vast amounts of energy during events such as solar flares or coronal mass ejections.

Observing the northern lights requires a combination of factors, including clear skies, darkness, and a bit of luck. The best time to view the aurora is during the winter months when nights are longest and the skies are darkest. Locations far from city lights offer the best opportunities, as light pollution can diminish the visibility of the aurora. Checking auroral forecasts, which predict geomagnetic activity based on solar observations, can help anticipate the best nights for viewing.

For those planning a trip to see the northern lights, preparation is key. Dressing warmly is essential, as the best viewing conditions often occur in frigid temperatures. Many northern regions offer guided tours, providing transportation to optimal viewing locations and insights from local experts. Setting up a camera with a tripod and using long-exposure settings can capture the vibrant colors and patterns of the aurora, preserving the memory of this magical experience.

The northern lights have long held cultural significance for indigenous peoples and local communities living in the Arctic regions. For the Sámi people of Scandinavia, the aurora borealis is woven into mythology and folklore, often seen as a spiritual presence or a manifestation of ancestral spirits. In some Inuit traditions, the lights are believed to be the spirits of ancestors playing in the sky, while other cultures regard them as omens or messages from the gods.

Scientific exploration of the northern lights dates back centuries, with early observations recorded by ancient civilizations. It wasn't until the 20th century that scientists began to understand the aurora's connection to solar activity and Earth's magnetic field. The advent of space exploration and satellite technology has provided further insights into the processes that drive the aurora, enhancing our understanding of space weather and its impact on Earth.

In recent years, the study of the aurora has expanded to include its effects on technology and communication systems. Geomagnetic storms can disrupt satellite operations, radio communications, and power grids, highlighting the need to monitor solar activity and develop strategies to mitigate these impacts. Understanding the aurora's interaction with Earth's magnetic field contributes to the broader field of space weather research, which aims to protect and enhance modern technological infrastructure.

For those captivated by the beauty and mystery of the northern lights, engaging with this phenomenon can take many forms. Amateur astronomers may track solar activity and geomagnetic conditions, while artists and photographers capture the aurora's vivid colors and dynamic movements. Educators can incorporate the science and cultural significance of the aurora into curricula, sparking curiosity and fostering a deeper connection to the natural world.

The northern lights serve as a reminder of the dynamic relationship between Earth and the sun, highlighting the interconnectedness of our solar system. They invite us to explore the boundaries of our understanding, inspiring a sense of wonder and discovery. As we gaze upon the luminous dance of the aurora borealis, we are reminded of the beauty and complexity of the universe, and the ever-present mysteries that await our exploration.

Comets Visitors from Afar

Comets, those enigmatic wanderers of the solar system, have long captivated the human imagination with their glowing tails and sporadic appearances. These icy bodies, often described as "dirty snowballs," travel vast distances through space, occasionally gracing our skies and offering us a glimpse into the distant reaches of our cosmic neighborhood. As visitors from afar, comets provide valuable insights into the early solar system, holding clues about its formation and evolution.

Composed primarily of ice, dust, and rocky material, comets originate from two main regions: the Kuiper Belt and the Oort Cloud. The Kuiper Belt is a disc-shaped region beyond Neptune's orbit, home to many short-period comets with orbits taking less than 200 years to complete. The Oort Cloud, a hypothetical spherical shell surrounding the solar system, is thought to be the birthplace of long-period comets, whose orbits can span thousands or even millions of years.

When a comet approaches the sun, the increase in temperature causes the ice within it to vaporize, releasing gas and dust. This process forms a glowing coma, a cloud of gas and dust that surrounds the comet's nucleus. Solar radiation and the solar wind then push the coma's materials away, forming the comet's characteristic tail. Remarkably, a comet can develop two distinct tails: a dust tail that glows in reflected sunlight and a gas or ion tail that fluoresces due to interactions with solar wind particles. The ion tail often points directly away from the sun due to these interactions.

Throughout history, comets have been regarded with awe and often fear, viewed as omens or harbingers of change. Ancient civilizations recorded comets in their chronicles, interpreting them through the lens of myth and superstition. The Great Comet of 1066, for instance, was seen as a portent of significant events, such as the Battle of Hastings. However, as our understanding of celestial phenomena grew, so did our perception of comets, shifting from mystical interpretations to scientific inquiry.

The scientific study of comets began to thrive in the 17th century, with astronomers such as Edmond Halley making significant contributions. Halley was the first to predict the return of a comet based on historical records, identifying the periodic nature of what would later be named Halley's Comet. His work laid the foundation for the study of cometary orbits and their role in the solar system.

Modern technology has enabled unprecedented exploration of comets. Space missions like the European Space Agency's Rosetta mission to Comet 67P/Churyumov-Gerasimenko have provided valuable data on the composition and behavior of these celestial bodies. Rosetta's lander, Philae, made history in 2014 by achieving the first-ever landing on a comet, revealing insights into its surface and subsurface composition.

The study of comets is not only a quest to understand these intriguing objects but also an exploration of our solar system's history. Comets are considered primordial building blocks, remnants from the early solar system that have remained relatively unchanged over billions of years. By analyzing the material within comets, scientists can glean information about the conditions present during the solar system's formation.

For amateur astronomers and enthusiasts, observing comets can be a rewarding experience. While some comets, like Halley's Comet, have predictable orbits and can be anticipated, others appear unexpectedly, offering a thrilling opportunity to witness their fleeting beauty. Comets can often be seen with the naked eye or through binoculars, depending on their brightness and proximity to Earth. Star charts and astronomical apps can aid in locating these transient visitors, enhancing the experience for observers.

Photographing comets requires some preparation and the right equipment. A camera with manual settings, a tripod, and a remote shutter release are essential for capturing long-exposure shots. Using a wide-angle lens can help frame the comet within the context of the night sky, while a telephoto lens can zoom in on the comet's details. Experimentation with exposure times and ISO settings can yield stunning images of the comet's nucleus and tails.

Beyond their visual appeal, comets have practical implications for planetary defense and space exploration. As remnants of the solar system's formation, they hold clues about volatile compounds and organic molecules that may have played a role in the development of life on Earth. Additionally, understanding cometary dynamics can contribute to mitigating potential threats posed by their unpredictable orbits. The study of comets may also inform future efforts to utilize their resources for space exploration, such as harvesting water ice for fuel or life support.

In cultural contexts, comets continue to inspire creativity and wonder. They appear in literature, art, and folklore, symbolizing everything from impending change to the continuity of the cosmos. Their ephemeral presence in the sky serves as a reminder of the vastness and complexity of the universe, inviting reflection on humanity's place within it.

Rare Celestial Alignments

Rare celestial alignments, those extraordinary moments when multiple astronomical bodies align with precision, have intrigued humanity for centuries.

These events, while infrequent, provide a unique glimpse into the harmonious mechanics of our solar system and beyond. From planetary conjunctions to syzygies involving the Earth, moon, and sun, these alignments offer not only breathtaking views but also opportunities for scientific discovery and cultural reflection.

A planetary conjunction occurs when two or more planets appear close together in the sky from Earth's perspective. These alignments are a result of the planets' orbits bringing them into similar lines of sight, creating a striking visual display. One of the most celebrated conjunctions is the Great Conjunction of Jupiter and Saturn, which occurs approximately every 20 years. In December 2020, this event captured global attention as the two gas giants appeared closer than they had in nearly 400 years, creating a bright, single point of light in the evening sky.

The rarity and beauty of such events often lead to cultural and historical significance. Throughout history, conjunctions have been interpreted as omens or signs, influencing decisions by leaders and inspiring myths. The Star of Bethlehem, for example, is speculated to have been a conjunction of bright planets, guiding the wise men according to Christian tradition.

An eclipse is a type of syzygy, an alignment involving the Earth, moon, and sun. Solar and lunar eclipses occur when these bodies align such that one is obscured by the shadow of another. While solar eclipses occur during a new moon, lunar eclipses happen during a full moon. These events have been well-documented throughout history, often associated with both awe and apprehension. Ancient civilizations meticulously recorded eclipses, using them to develop early astronomical models and calendars.

Another fascinating alignment involves transits, when a smaller celestial body passes directly across the face of a larger one from the observer's viewpoint. The transit of Venus across the sun is a rare occurrence, happening in pairs separated by over a century. The last transits took place in 2004 and 2012, and the next will not occur until 2117. Historically, transits of Venus were crucial for astronomers in the 18th and 19th centuries to measure the astronomical unit, the average distance between the Earth and the sun, helping refine our understanding of the solar system's scale.

Beyond our solar system, celestial alignments can reveal the presence of exoplanets through the transit method. As a planet passes in front of its host star, it causes a temporary dip in the star's brightness, which can be detected by telescopes. This technique has led to the discovery of thousands of exoplanets, expanding our knowledge of planetary systems beyond our own and challenging our understanding of planet formation and habitability.

For amateur astronomers, observing rare celestial alignments requires preparation and patience. Selecting an appropriate location with a clear, unobstructed view of the sky is crucial, as is timing the observation to coincide with the alignment's peak. Tools such as star charts, astronomy apps, and telescopes can enhance the experience, allowing observers to appreciate the full spectacle of these events.

Photographing celestial alignments can be a rewarding endeavor, capturing the ephemeral beauty of these cosmic dances. A camera with manual settings and a tripod is essential for long-exposure photography, enabling the capture of detail and color in the night sky. Experimenting with different lenses and exposure settings can yield stunning images that preserve the memory of these rare occurrences.

Celestial alignments also serve as opportunities for scientific study, contributing to our understanding of gravitational dynamics, orbital mechanics, and the broader workings of the universe. By studying these events, scientists can refine models of celestial motion, test theories of relativity, and explore the interactions between celestial bodies. The data collected during alignments can illuminate the complexities of planetary atmospheres, magnetic fields, and other phenomena that might otherwise remain hidden.

Culturally, rare celestial alignments continue to inspire art, literature, and philosophy, prompting reflection on humanity's place in the cosmos. They remind us of the delicate balance and interconnectedness of the universe, evoking wonder and curiosity. These alignments challenge us to look beyond our immediate surroundings and ponder the vastness of space and time, inviting exploration and discovery.

As we advance in our exploration of the cosmos, the study and observation of celestial alignments remain a vital aspect of astronomy. They connect us to the rhythms of the universe, offering a tangible link to the celestial mechanics that govern our solar system. Whether through scientific inquiry or personal reflection, these rare events enrich our understanding of the natural world and inspire a sense of unity with the cosmos.

Chapter 4: Mapping the Night Sky

Constellations Legends and Locations

For centuries, constellations have been humanity's celestial companions, guiding travelers, inspiring storytellers, and serving as the canvas upon which cultures have projected their myths and legends. These star patterns, visible from Earth, are not only navigational tools but also windows into the rich tapestry of human history and imagination. By understanding the legends and locations associated with these constellations, we can appreciate the intricate ways in which the night sky has shaped and reflected human experience.

The constellations we recognize today are steeped in mythology, their stories woven into the fabric of ancient cultures. The Greeks, for instance, bequeathed us many of the constellations we know, linking them to tales of gods, heroes, and creatures. Orion, the Hunter, is one of the most prominent. His story is one of might and tragedy, often associated with his unrequited love for Artemis, the goddess of the hunt, and his eventual placement in the sky by the gods. Orion's easily recognizable belt of three stars serves as a celestial landmark, guiding stargazers to other neighboring constellations.

Similarly, the constellation of Perseus carries the narrative of the hero's daring rescue of Andromeda, depicted in the sky alongside her parents, Cepheus and Cassiopeia. This celestial family illustrates the Greek penchant for immortalizing their myths among the stars, creating a cosmic theater where tales of bravery and folly play out night after night.

The ancient Egyptians also found meaning in the stars, aligning their pyramids with the constellations. They associated Orion with Osiris, the god of the afterlife, believing that the constellation's alignment with the Nile's flooding heralded the renewal of life. Such connections between earthly events and celestial patterns highlight the profound influence constellations have had on human civilization, linking the rhythms of the heavens with the cycles of life on Earth.

In the Southern Hemisphere, indigenous cultures have their own rich traditions of star lore. The Aboriginal Australians, for example, have long used constellations for navigation and storytelling. The Emu in the Sky, formed by dark dust lanes in the Milky Way rather than bright stars, reflects their unique perspective on the cosmos. This figure, visible from April to October, is associated with lore about creation, law, and the natural world, demonstrating how constellations can convey cultural values and knowledge.

For beginners interested in locating constellations, understanding their seasonal appearances is key. The night sky changes with the Earth's orbit around the sun, bringing different constellations into view throughout the year. In the Northern Hemisphere, winter skies reveal Orion, Taurus, and Gemini, while summer brings the Summer Triangle, composed of the bright stars Vega, Deneb, and Altair, which are part of the constellations Lyra, Cygnus, and Aquila, respectively. Meanwhile, Southern Hemisphere stargazers can enjoy the Southern Cross, a prominent constellation that serves as a navigational aid.

Stargazing requires little more than a clear night and an unobstructed view of the sky. However, a star chart or a stargazing app can enhance the experience, helping to identify constellations and their myths. As your eyes adjust to the darkness, more stars will become visible, revealing the constellations' full splendor. Binoculars or a small telescope can further enrich the experience, bringing fainter stars and deep-sky objects into view.

Constellations also play a vital role in modern astronomy, serving as a framework for mapping the sky. The International Astronomical Union officially recognizes 88 constellations, dividing the celestial sphere into defined areas. While the stars within these constellations are not physically related, their apparent proximity from Earth creates patterns that help astronomers navigate and categorize the night sky.

Beyond their scientific utility, constellations continue to inspire artists, writers, and dreamers. They invite us to connect with the past, to imagine the stories told by our ancestors, and to create new narratives that reflect our own experiences and aspirations. Whether through poetry, visual art, or music, constellations offer a wellspring of inspiration that transcends time and culture.

Engaging with constellations can also foster a sense of connection with the natural world. In an age of urbanization and technology, stargazing provides a moment of reflection and wonder, reminding us of the vastness of the universe and our place within it. As we trace the outlines of familiar star patterns, we participate in a timeless tradition shared by countless generations, bridging the gap between the past and the present.

Using Star Charts and Apps

Navigating the night sky can be a daunting task for beginners, but with the right tools, it becomes an exhilarating journey of discovery. Star charts and apps serve as invaluable guides, transforming a seemingly chaotic expanse of stars into a comprehensible map of the cosmos. By learning to use these tools effectively, one can quickly become adept at identifying constellations, planets, and deep-sky objects, enhancing the stargazing experience.

Star charts are traditional tools that have been used for centuries to map the heavens. These maps, often circular in design, depict the night sky as seen from a specific latitude at a particular time of year. They are printed with constellations, stars, and other celestial objects, providing a snapshot of the sky's configuration. To use a star chart, one typically aligns it with the cardinal directions, matching the chart's orientation with the real-world compass points. This alignment helps to accurately represent the sky above, allowing users to locate specific stars and constellations.

For those new to stargazing, understanding how to read a star chart is crucial. The chart's outer edge often includes a calendar that correlates with the months of the year. By rotating the chart to align the current date with the time of night, users can see a representation of the sky at that particular moment. This feature is especially helpful in accounting for the sky's changing appearance as Earth orbits the sun.

While star charts provide a tactile and traditional method of navigating the night sky, modern technology offers digital alternatives that are equally powerful. Astronomy apps have revolutionized the way we explore the cosmos, providing an interactive and accessible platform for stargazers of all levels. These apps, available for smartphones and tablets, use augmented reality to superimpose star maps over the real sky. By simply pointing a device at the sky, users can instantly identify celestial objects and learn more about them.

One of the most significant advantages of using apps is their dynamic nature. They can provide real-time updates on celestial events, offer detailed information about stars and planets, and even simulate the night sky from different locations and times. This versatility makes apps an excellent learning tool, allowing users to explore the universe beyond what is visible to the naked eye.

Choosing the right app can enhance the stargazing experience. Many apps offer features such as detailed star maps, information on upcoming astronomical events, and even guided tours of the night sky. Some popular options include SkySafari, Stellarium, and

Star Walk, each offering unique features tailored to different user preferences. When selecting an app, consider its user interface, available features, and compatibility with your device.

For beginners, combining the use of star charts and apps can be particularly beneficial. Star charts provide a foundational understanding of the sky's layout, fostering a deeper connection to the traditional methods of celestial navigation. Meanwhile, apps offer a dynamic and interactive experience, making it easier to learn and explore. Together, these tools create a comprehensive approach to stargazing, blending the old with the new.

To maximize the stargazing experience, consider the conditions under which you'll be observing. Light pollution can significantly impact visibility, so finding a dark location away from city lights is ideal. Allowing time for your eyes to adjust to the darkness enhances your ability to see faint stars and celestial objects. Patience and practice are key, as familiarity with the night sky grows over time.

Engaging with star charts and apps also opens the door to the broader community of astronomy enthusiasts. Many local astronomy clubs and online forums offer resources, events, and support for beginners. Participating in star parties or guided nights under the stars can provide valuable insights, as experienced astronomers share their knowledge and passion for the cosmos.

Beyond practical applications, using star charts and apps fosters a deeper appreciation for the universe. These tools not only guide us through the night sky but also connect us to the rich history of astronomical exploration. They remind us of humanity's enduring fascination with the stars and our desire to understand our place within the cosmos.

Navigating the Sky by Seasons

The sky, an ever-changing tapestry above, offers a celestial performance that varies with the seasons. Each season brings a unique set of constellations, celestial events, and atmospheric conditions. Mastering the art of seasonal sky navigation enhances one's stargazing experience, providing both amateur astronomers and seasoned sky enthusiasts a deeper understanding of the cosmos.

Spring nights usher in a gentle warmth, waking the heavens from their winter slumber. As the earth tilts toward the sun, the constellations of Leo, Virgo, and Ursa Major dominate the night sky. Leo, the lion, prowls the heavens with its distinct sickle-shaped mane. This constellation serves as a guidepost to nearby galaxies, such as the Leo Triplet, a trio of spiraling galaxies visible through modest telescopes. Virgo, with its bright star Spica, heralds the spring equinox. The Virgo Cluster, a massive collection of galaxies, lies within this constellation, offering a glimpse into the universe's vastness. Ursa Major, the Great Bear, never dips below the horizon in the northern hemisphere. Its seven brightest stars form the Big Dipper, a crucial navigational tool pointing toward Polaris, the North Star.

Summer brings longer days and shorter nights, but the sky remains a treasure trove for observers. The Summer Triangle, a prominent asterism, marks the season. This celestial trio consists of Vega in Lyra, Altair in Aquila, and Deneb in Cygnus. Vega, one of the brightest stars in the sky, serves as a beacon for summer stargazers. Lyra, home to the Ring Nebula, offers a stunning planetary nebula visible through small telescopes. Altair, the swift-winged eagle of Aquila, soars high, while Deneb, a supergiant, anchors the tail of Cygnus, the swan. Together, these stars create a celestial triangle, guiding the observer's eye to the heart of the Milky Way.

Autumn nights, crisp and clear, unveil a different celestial story. The constellations of Pegasus, Andromeda, and Cassiopeia take center stage. Pegasus, the winged horse, gallops across the sky with its square body. The Great Square of Pegasus acts as a gateway to the Andromeda Galaxy, the nearest spiral galaxy to our own. Andromeda, named after the mythical princess, stretches across the sky, accompanied by the faint glow of its namesake galaxy. Cassiopeia, the celestial queen, forms a distinct W shape, a reliable marker for navigating the autumn sky. Her throne sits near the radiant Perseus, providing a starting point for meteor showers like the Perseids.

Winter nights, though cold and brisk, offer some of the clearest skies for observation. Orion, the mighty hunter, dominates the winter sky with his gleaming belt of three stars. Betelgeuse, a red supergiant, marks his shoulder, while Rigel, a blue supergiant, shines at his foot. The Orion Nebula, a stellar nursery, beckons observers with its wispy tendrils visible through binoculars. Canis Major, the great dog, faithfully follows Orion, with Sirius, the brightest star in the night sky, leading the way. Taurus, the bull, charges across the heavens, its eye represented by the fiery Aldebaran. The Pleiades, a cluster of young stars, rest on the bull's back, appearing like a delicate jewel box through telescopes.

Celestial events punctuate the seasons, offering additional spectacles. Spring hosts the Lyrid meteor shower, with bright streaks darting across the sky. Summer boasts the Perseids, often producing over a hundred meteors per hour. Autumn brings the Draconids, a more erratic but occasionally brilliant display. Winter concludes with the Geminids, known for their multi-colored meteors. These events, predictable yet ephemeral, connect us to the rhythms of the cosmos.

Atmospheric conditions also vary by season, influencing sky observation. Spring and autumn often provide the clearest skies, as the transitional weather patterns minimize atmospheric turbulence. Summer's warmth can lead to hazy skies, while winter's chill often results in crisp, transparent nights. Understanding these seasonal shifts aids in planning optimal stargazing experiences.

Light pollution, an ever-present challenge, affects visibility differently with each season. Urban observers might find winter's long nights advantageous, while rural stargazers enjoy summer's brief but dark intervals. Awareness and adaptation to light pollution enhance the ability to navigate the seasonal sky effectively.

Equipment choice aligns with seasonal changes. Spring's galaxies and nebulae invite the use of telescopes, while summer's wide-field views benefit from binoculars. Autumn's crisp air allows for detailed observations, while winter's cold necessitates protective gear for both observer and equipment. Adapting tools and techniques to the season maximizes the celestial bounty each period offers.

Cultural and historical contexts enrich the experience of seasonal sky navigation. Many ancient civilizations relied on the stars for agricultural and navigational purposes, embedding them deeply in myth and lore. Understanding these stories adds depth to the practice of stargazing, transforming it from a solitary pursuit into a shared human experience across time.

The Zodiac and Its Influence

The zodiac, a celestial belt in the sky, has fascinated humanity for millennia, weaving its way into the fabric of cultures, beliefs, and practices across the globe. Comprised of twelve distinct constellations, each associated with a specific time of the year, the zodiac offers insights into the movement of celestial bodies and the influence they are believed to exert on earthly affairs.

The origins of the zodiac can be traced back to ancient Babylonian astronomy, where early astronomers divided the sky into twelve equal segments, each corresponding to a constellation. These segments, or zodiac signs, became a critical component of the Babylonian calendar, aiding in agricultural cycles and religious ceremonies. As this knowledge spread through trade and conquest, the Greeks adopted and refined the Babylonian system, integrating their mythology and philosophy. This synthesis laid the foundation for the zodiac as we understand it today.

Each zodiac sign is associated with specific traits, elements, and planetary rulers, contributing to its unique influence. Aries, the ram, heralds the arrival of spring with its fiery energy and bold determination. Ruled by Mars, Aries embodies the pioneering spirit, often associated with leadership and courage. Taurus, the bull, represents stability and sensuality, governed by Venus, the planet of love and beauty. Its earthy nature grounds the zodiac, emphasizing practicality and perseverance.

Gemini, the twins, brings adaptability and communication, ruled by Mercury, the messenger of the gods. This air sign thrives on intellectual stimulation and social interaction, epitomizing curiosity and versatility. Cancer, the crab, offers nurturing and emotional depth, under the influence of the moon. Its water element fosters intuition and empathy, creating a protective and caring presence.

Leo, the lion, radiates confidence and creativity, governed by the sun. This fire sign exudes warmth and charisma, inspiring others with its enthusiasm and passion. Virgo, the maiden, embodies precision and analytical skills, with Mercury as its ruler. An earth sign, Virgo values organization and service, often seeking perfection in its pursuits.

Libra, the scales, balances harmony and justice, influenced by Venus. As an air sign, Libra prioritizes relationships and aesthetics, striving for peace and equilibrium. Scorpio, the scorpion, delves into transformation and intensity, ruled by both Mars and Pluto. Its water element fosters resilience and resourcefulness, navigating the depths of emotion and change.

Sagittarius, the archer, embodies exploration and optimism, guided by Jupiter, the planet of expansion. This fire sign seeks knowledge and adventure, constantly pushing boundaries and embracing growth. Capricorn, the goat, represents ambition and discipline, with Saturn as its ruler. An earth sign, Capricorn values structure and achievement, working diligently toward its goals.

Aquarius, the water bearer, champions innovation and independence, influenced by Uranus and Saturn. As an air sign, Aquarius promotes progressive thinking and humanitarian efforts, often challenging the status quo. Pisces, the fish, offers compassion and imagination, ruled by both Jupiter and Neptune. Its water element nurtures creativity and spirituality, inviting introspection and connection.

Astrology, the study of celestial influences on human affairs, positions the zodiac at its core. Astrologers interpret the positions of the sun, moon, and planets within the zodiac to create horoscopes, personalized guides that suggest tendencies, challenges, and opportunities. These interpretations often consider the elements, modalities, and planetary aspects, creating a complex and nuanced picture.

The elements—fire, earth, air, and water—categorize the zodiac signs, each contributing distinct characteristics. Fire signs (Aries, Leo, Sagittarius) embody passion, energy, and dynamism. Earth signs (Taurus, Virgo, Capricorn) offer stability, practicality, and reliability. Air signs (Gemini, Libra, Aquarius) emphasize intellect, communication, and adaptability. Water signs (Cancer, Scorpio, Pisces) bring emotional depth, intuition, and sensitivity.

Modalities—cardinal, fixed, and mutable—further define the signs' approaches to change and action. Cardinal signs (Aries, Cancer, Libra, Capricorn) initiate and lead, often taking charge in new situations. Fixed signs (Taurus, Leo, Scorpio, Aquarius) provide stability and persistence, maintaining focus and dedication. Mutable signs (Gemini, Virgo, Sagittarius, Pisces) adapt and transform, embracing flexibility and evolution.

The planets' positions and aspects within the zodiac influence individual and collective experiences. For example, a conjunction, where two planets align closely, often amplifies their combined energies. A square, a 90-degree angle, may indicate tension or challenges, prompting growth and resolution. A trine, a 120-degree angle, suggests harmony and ease, facilitating cooperation and success.

Despite its ancient roots, the zodiac remains relevant in contemporary culture. Its symbols and meanings permeate art, literature, and popular media, offering archetypal narratives and insights. Astrology, while both revered and critiqued, continues to captivate those seeking guidance and connection, reflecting the enduring human desire to understand our place in the cosmos.

Engaging with the zodiac invites introspection and exploration, encouraging individuals to consider their strengths, challenges, and potential paths. Whether approached as a belief system, a cultural artifact, or a tool for self-reflection, the zodiac offers a rich tapestry of symbolism and meaning, inviting curiosity and contemplation.

The Art of Astrophotography

Capturing the grandeur of the cosmos through astrophotography is a pursuit that marries technical skill with artistic vision. It demands patience, precision, and an understanding of both the night sky and the tools used to immortalize its beauty. For beginners, the journey into astrophotography can seem daunting, yet with the right guidance and approach, it unfolds as a deeply rewarding adventure.

Astrophotography begins with the choice of equipment. While the allure of advanced cameras and telescopes is strong, starting with a DSLR or mirrorless camera and a sturdy tripod provides a solid foundation. These cameras, with their ability to manually adjust settings such as shutter speed, aperture, and ISO, offer the flexibility needed to capture faint celestial objects. A lens with a wide aperture, such as f/2.8 or faster, allows more light to reach the camera sensor, which is crucial for photographing dim stars and nebulae.

Location is paramount in astrophotography. Light pollution from urban areas washes out the night sky, obscuring all but the brightest stars. To achieve the best results, seek out dark sky locations, far from city lights. These areas, often designated as Dark Sky Parks or Reserves, provide the ideal conditions for capturing the cosmos in all its splendor. Planning a shoot around the new moon ensures the darkest skies, as moonlight can also interfere with long-exposure photography.

Once the equipment and location are set, mastering the camera settings becomes essential. In astrophotography, long exposures are key. By leaving the camera shutter open for extended periods, more light from distant stars and galaxies is captured. However, too long of an exposure can lead to star trails, where stars appear to streak across the image due to Earth's rotation. The 500 Rule provides a useful guideline: divide 500 by the focal length of the lens to determine the maximum exposure time in seconds before trails become noticeable.

Focus is another critical aspect. Autofocus is often ineffective in low-light conditions, so manual focusing is necessary. Set the camera to live view mode and zoom in on a bright star or distant light source. Adjust the focus ring until the star appears as a sharp point of light. This ensures that the entire field of view is in focus, capturing the intricate details of the night sky.

Astrophotography is not limited to wide-field shots of the Milky Way or constellations. With the right equipment, planetary photography and deep-sky imaging become possible. A telescope with a motorized mount, capable of tracking the movement of the sky, allows for longer exposures without star trails, enabling the capture of planets, star clusters, and nebulae. Specialized astrophotography cameras, often cooled to reduce sensor noise, enhance the clarity and detail of these images.

Post-processing plays a significant role in astrophotography, transforming raw images into breathtaking vistas of the cosmos. Software such as Adobe Lightroom or Photoshop allows photographers to adjust exposure, contrast, and color balance, bringing out the hidden details in their shots. Techniques like stacking, where multiple images of the same subject are combined to reduce noise and increase detail, are particularly useful for deep-sky objects.

Astrophotography also offers an opportunity to experiment with different styles and compositions. Time-lapse photography, for instance, captures the movement of stars across the sky, creating dynamic videos that reveal the passage of time. Light painting, where artificial light sources are used to illuminate foreground objects during a long exposure, adds depth and context to night sky images.

Each astrophotographer brings a unique perspective to their work, influenced by personal interests, location, and equipment. Some may focus on capturing the grandeur of the Milky Way, while others might seek out distant galaxies or the intricate details of the moon's surface. This diversity of approaches contributes to a rich tapestry of images that showcase the beauty and complexity of the universe.

Astrophotography is a journey of discovery, both of the cosmos and of one's own creative potential. It requires a blend of technical proficiency and artistic intuition, as well as a willingness to embrace the challenges and unpredictability of working with the night sky. For those who persevere, the rewards are profound—an opportunity to capture and share the awe-inspiring beauty of the universe, and a deeper connection to the celestial wonders that have fascinated humanity for centuries.

Embarking on this journey requires patience and a commitment to continuous learning. Each outing offers lessons, whether in understanding how different atmospheric conditions affect image quality or in mastering the intricacies of post-processing. Engaging with the astrophotography community, through online forums and local clubs, provides valuable insights and fosters a sense of camaraderie among those who share a passion for capturing the stars.

Chapter 5: The Science Behind the Stars

Understanding Light and Distance

Light, the messenger of the cosmos, travels vast distances to reach us, carrying with it the secrets of distant stars, galaxies, and nebulae. Understanding the interplay between light and distance is essential for anyone seeking to unlock the mysteries of the universe. This chapter delves into the fundamental concepts of light and distance, providing a foundation for beginners eager to explore the cosmos.

At its core, light is electromagnetic radiation, visible to the human eye as a spectrum of colors. It travels at a staggering speed of approximately 299,792 kilometers per second (about 186,282 miles per second) in a vacuum. This speed, a universal constant, allows light to cover immense distances, revealing the universe's grandeur and complexity. The time it takes for light to travel from a celestial object to Earth is referred to as a light year, a measure of distance rather than time. One light year is the distance light travels in one year, approximately 9.46 trillion kilometers (about 5.88 trillion miles).

The concept of light years introduces a fascinating aspect of astronomical observation: when we observe distant celestial objects, we are essentially looking back in time. The light from the nearest star system, Alpha Centauri, takes over four years to reach us, meaning we see it as it was four years ago. This time-traveling aspect of light allows astronomers to study the universe's history, observing galaxies and stars as they were millions or even billions of years in the past.

The journey of light is not always straightforward. As it travels through space, it can be absorbed, scattered, or refracted by interstellar dust and gas. These interactions can alter the light's path and characteristics, providing valuable information about the medium it traversed. For instance, the reddening of light as it passes through dust clouds indicates the presence of certain elements and compounds, enabling astronomers to deduce the composition of distant regions of space.

Wavelength, a key property of light, determines its color and energy. Light with shorter wavelengths, such as blue and violet, carries more energy than light with longer wavelengths, like red and infrared. This principle is crucial in understanding phenomena such as redshift and blueshift, which occur when celestial objects move relative to the observer. An object moving away from us causes its light to shift toward the red end of the spectrum, a phenomenon known as redshift. Conversely, an object moving closer causes a blueshift. These shifts provide critical insights into the motion and expansion of the universe, as exemplified by the observation that distant galaxies are moving away from us, suggesting an expanding cosmos.

The inverse square law is another principle that governs the behavior of light over distance. According to this law, the intensity of light diminishes with the square of the distance from its source. This means that as light travels farther from its origin, it spreads out and becomes fainter. This phenomenon affects the brightness of celestial objects as observed from Earth, necessitating the use of more powerful telescopes and sensitive instruments to detect faint or distant sources of light.

Telescopes, the primary tools for observing light from distant objects, come in various forms. Refracting telescopes use lenses to bend and focus light, while reflecting telescopes employ mirrors to achieve the same purpose. Each type has its advantages and limitations, but both are designed to gather as much light as possible, enhancing the visibility of celestial objects. The aperture size, or the diameter of the primary lens or mirror, is a critical factor in determining a telescope's light-gathering ability. Larger apertures collect more light, allowing for clearer and more detailed observations of faint and distant objects.

Space-based telescopes, such as the Hubble Space Telescope, offer an unparalleled view of the universe by operating above Earth's atmosphere, which can distort and absorb light. These instruments capture light across a range of wavelengths, from ultraviolet to infrared, revealing details that ground-based observatories might miss. The ability to observe in different wavelengths is crucial, as many celestial phenomena emit light outside the visible spectrum. For example, infrared observations can penetrate dust clouds to reveal star-forming regions, while ultraviolet light highlights the energetic processes of young stars and active galaxies.

Astronomers also rely on spectroscopy, the study of light's interaction with matter, to glean information about celestial objects. By analyzing the spectrum of light emitted or absorbed by an object, scientists can determine its composition, temperature, density, and motion. Spectroscopy has led to groundbreaking discoveries, such as the identification of exoplanet atmospheres and the confirmation of dark matter's existence.

Understanding the relationship between light and distance extends beyond professional astronomy to everyday stargazing. Recognizing that the stars we see are at varying distances helps us appreciate the vastness of the universe and the scale of cosmic events. It also emphasizes the importance of patience and perseverance in astronomical observation, as capturing the faintest glimmers of light often requires long exposures and careful analysis.

Spectroscopy Unlocking Star Secrets

Spectroscopy, an indispensable tool in modern astronomy, serves as a key to unlocking the secrets of stars and other celestial bodies. By analyzing the light emitted or absorbed by these distant objects, scientists can decipher clues about their composition, temperature, motion, and more. This chapter delves into the intricacies of spectroscopy, providing beginners with a comprehensive understanding of its principles and applications in the study of the cosmos.

At its essence, spectroscopy involves the dispersion of light into its constituent wavelengths, creating a spectrum. This spectrum acts as a fingerprint, unique to each astronomical object, revealing vital information about its physical and chemical properties. The foundation of spectroscopy lies in the understanding of light as both a wave and a particle, a dual nature that enables it to interact with matter in diverse ways.

When light from a star or other celestial source passes through a prism or a diffraction grating, it is separated into a spectrum of colors, each corresponding to a specific wavelength. This spectrum can be continuous, emission, or absorption, each type providing distinct information. A continuous spectrum, like that of a blackbody, displays an unbroken range of colors, indicative of the object's temperature. Emission spectra, characterized by bright lines on a dark background, arise when atoms or molecules in an excited state release energy in the form of light. Absorption spectra, on the other hand, show dark lines superimposed on a continuous spectrum, resulting from specific wavelengths of light being absorbed by atoms or molecules in a cooler, intervening medium.

The study of these spectral lines, first systematically examined by German physicist Gustav Kirchhoff and chemist Robert Bunsen in the 19th century, laid the groundwork for modern spectroscopy. They discovered that each chemical element produces a unique set of spectral lines, acting as a barcode for its identification. This breakthrough allowed astronomers to determine the composition of stars and other celestial bodies, even those light-years away.

One of the most significant applications of spectroscopy in astronomy is the determination of stellar composition. By comparing the spectral lines observed in a star's light with those produced by elements on Earth, astronomers can identify the elements present in the star's atmosphere. This process has revealed that stars, including our sun, are primarily composed of hydrogen and helium, with trace amounts of heavier elements. This knowledge has been instrumental in understanding stellar evolution, nucleosynthesis, and the broader chemical evolution of the universe.

Spectroscopy also provides insights into the temperature of stars. The shape and intensity of a star's spectrum are influenced by its surface temperature, a relationship described by Planck's law of blackbody radiation. Hotter stars emit more light at shorter wavelengths, resulting in a bluer appearance, while cooler stars emit more at longer wavelengths, appearing redder. By analyzing the spectrum, astronomers can estimate a star's temperature and classify it accordingly, contributing to the development of the Hertzsprung-Russell diagram, a pivotal tool for understanding stellar lifecycles.

Motion, another critical aspect of celestial objects, can be inferred through spectroscopy via the Doppler effect. When a star or galaxy moves relative to an observer, its spectral lines shift in wavelength. A shift toward longer wavelengths, known as redshift, indicates the object is moving away, while a shift toward shorter wavelengths, or blueshift, suggests it is approaching. This phenomenon has been instrumental in measuring the velocities of stars, the rotation rates of galaxies, and the expansion of the universe itself, leading to groundbreaking discoveries such as Hubble's law and the Big Bang theory.

In addition to stars, spectroscopy has been pivotal in studying other astronomical phenomena, such as nebulae, quasars, and exoplanets. The spectra of nebulae, for instance, reveal the presence of ionized gases and dust, providing insights into the processes of star formation and the recycling of stellar material. Quasars, the luminous cores of distant galaxies, exhibit highly redshifted spectra, offering a glimpse into the early universe and the growth of supermassive black holes.

Exoplanet research has also been revolutionized by spectroscopy. When an exoplanet transits its host star, some of the star's light passes through the planet's atmosphere, imprinting spectral signatures that can be analyzed to identify atmospheric components. This technique has led to the detection of water vapor, carbon dioxide, and other molecules in exoplanet atmospheres, advancing our understanding of planetary systems and the potential for life beyond Earth.

The development of sophisticated spectroscopic instruments, both ground-based and spaceborne, has expanded the reach and precision of these investigations. Instruments such as the Hubble Space Telescope's Cosmic Origins Spectrograph and the European Southern Observatory's Very Large Telescope have enabled astronomers to obtain high-resolution spectra of faint and distant objects, pushing the boundaries of our cosmic knowledge.

For beginners, engaging with spectroscopy offers an opportunity to appreciate the interconnectedness of light, matter, and motion in the universe. It encourages a deeper exploration of the physical principles that govern celestial phenomena and fosters a greater appreciation for the ingenuity and creativity involved in scientific discovery.

The Role of Telescopes in Discovery

Telescopes stand as one of humanity's most profound inventions, extending our vision beyond the confines of Earth and into the vast expanse of the universe. They have played a pivotal role in astronomical discovery, transforming our understanding of the cosmos and our place within it. From the simple refracting telescopes of the Renaissance to the sophisticated space observatories of today, these instruments have continually pushed the boundaries of what we can observe and comprehend.

The journey of telescopic discovery began in the early 17th century with Galileo Galilei, who, inspired by reports of a Dutch invention, crafted his own telescope. With this modest instrument, Galileo peered into the night sky and unveiled wonders never before seen by human eyes. He discovered the four largest moons of Jupiter, observed the phases of Venus, and identified the rugged topography of the moon. These revelations challenged the prevailing geocentric model of the universe, laying the groundwork for a new understanding of celestial mechanics.

As telescopes evolved, so too did their capacity to reveal the universe's intricacies. The development of the reflecting telescope by Sir Isaac Newton marked a significant advancement, utilizing mirrors instead of lenses to gather and focus light. This innovation allowed for larger apertures, thereby increasing the telescope's light-gathering power and providing clearer, more detailed images. With these advancements, astronomers were able to explore deeper into space, discovering new planets, stars, and galaxies.

The 19th and 20th centuries witnessed a surge in telescopic discoveries, driven by technological advancements and the construction of larger and more powerful observatories. The 100-inch Hooker Telescope at Mount Wilson Observatory played a crucial role in Edwin Hubble's groundbreaking discovery of the expanding universe. By observing the redshift of galaxies, Hubble provided compelling evidence that the universe was not static but dynamic, leading to the formulation of the Big Bang theory.

Radio telescopes, introduced in the 1930s, opened a new window to the universe by detecting radio waves emitted by celestial objects. This leap allowed astronomers to study phenomena invisible to optical telescopes, such as pulsars, quasars, and cosmic microwave background radiation. The discovery of pulsars in the 1960s, for instance, provided insights into the life cycles of stars and the behavior of matter under extreme conditions.

Space-based telescopes have further revolutionized our exploration of the cosmos. Free from the distortion and absorption of Earth's atmosphere, these observatories capture clear, high-resolution images across a range of wavelengths, from gamma rays to infrared. The Hubble Space Telescope, launched in 1990, has become an iconic symbol of astronomical achievement, revealing the beauty and complexity of the universe through its stunning images. It has contributed to our understanding of black holes, the formation of galaxies, and the acceleration of cosmic expansion.

The James Webb Space Telescope, set to succeed Hubble, promises to delve even deeper into the universe's past, exploring the formation of the first stars and galaxies. Its advanced infrared capabilities will allow astronomers to peer through cosmic dust clouds, uncovering hidden star-forming regions and studying the atmospheres of exoplanets in unprecedented detail.

Telescopes have also played a crucial role in the discovery and characterization of exoplanets. Ground-based observatories, equipped with sensitive spectrographs, have detected the subtle wobbles of stars caused by the gravitational pull of orbiting planets. Space missions like Kepler and TESS have identified thousands of exoplanets by monitoring the tiny dips in starlight as planets transit their host stars. These discoveries have expanded our understanding of planetary systems and the potential for life beyond Earth.

The role of telescopes in discovery extends beyond professional astronomy to amateur astronomers and enthusiasts. With advancements in technology and the availability of affordable telescopes, countless individuals have taken to the night sky, contributing to discoveries such as comets, asteroids, and variable stars. Organizations like the American Association of Variable Star Observers harness the power of citizen science, encouraging amateurs to participate in data collection and analysis.

Telescopes are not merely instruments of observation; they are catalysts for curiosity and inspiration. They invite us to ponder the mysteries of the universe, to question our assumptions, and to seek answers beyond the horizon. Each discovery, whether a distant galaxy or a nearby exoplanet, adds a layer of richness to our understanding of the cosmos, challenging us to explore further and dream bigger.

As we continue to develop more advanced telescopes, both on Earth and in space, the potential for discovery is boundless. Projects like the Square Kilometre Array and the Extremely Large Telescope promise to transform our understanding of the universe's structure and evolution, probing the unknown with unprecedented sensitivity and precision.

Gravitational Waves and Their Insights

The discovery of gravitational waves marked a groundbreaking moment in our understanding of the universe, opening a new window through which we can observe cosmic phenomena. These ripples in the fabric of spacetime, first predicted by Albert Einstein over a century ago, provide insights into some of the universe's most cataclysmic events. The detection of gravitational waves not only confirmed a key prediction of Einstein's general theory of relativity but also ushered in a new era of astrophysics, where we can "hear" the universe in a way that was previously unimaginable.

Gravitational waves are generated by the acceleration of massive objects, such as merging black holes or neutron stars. As these objects move, they create distortions in spacetime that propagate outward at the speed of light, similar to how a pebble creates ripples when dropped into a pond. These waves carry information about their origins, providing a direct means to observe and study phenomena that emit little to no electromagnetic radiation.

The first direct detection of gravitational waves occurred on September 14, 2015, by the Laser Interferometer Gravitational-Wave Observatory (LIGO). The signal, known as GW150914, originated from the merger of two black holes, each about 30 times the mass of the sun, located approximately 1.3 billion light-years away. This historic event not only confirmed the existence of gravitational waves but also provided the first direct evidence of binary black hole systems, shedding light on the population and properties of these enigmatic objects.

The detection of gravitational waves requires incredibly sensitive instruments, as these waves are minuscule by the time they reach Earth. LIGO, for instance, is designed to detect changes in length smaller than a proton over a distance of four kilometers. It achieves this sensitivity by using laser beams to measure the minute distortions in spacetime caused by passing gravitational waves. The observatory's twin facilities, located in Louisiana and Washington, work in tandem to ensure that detected signals are indeed from gravitational waves and not local disturbances.

Since the initial detection, LIGO, in collaboration with the Virgo observatory in Europe, has identified several more gravitational wave events. These detections have included additional black hole mergers and, notably, the merger of two neutron stars, observed on August 17, 2017, as GW170817. This event was particularly significant because it was accompanied by electromagnetic signals across the spectrum, from gamma rays to radio waves. The simultaneous observation of gravitational and electromagnetic waves from the same source marked the dawn of multi-messenger astronomy, allowing scientists to study the event from multiple perspectives and gain a more comprehensive understanding of the processes involved.

Gravitational wave astronomy offers unique insights into the universe's most extreme conditions. Black holes and neutron stars, the primary sources of detectable gravitational waves, are remnants of massive stars that have undergone gravitational collapse. Studying these objects through their gravitational wave emissions provides information about their masses, spins, and distances, as well as the environments in which they formed and evolved.

One of the most intriguing aspects of gravitational wave detection is its potential to probe the early universe. Unlike electromagnetic radiation, which can be absorbed or scattered by matter, gravitational waves travel unimpeded through space, carrying information from the very moments after the Big Bang. Although current detectors are not sensitive enough to observe these primordial waves, future observatories like the proposed space-based Laser Interferometer Space Antenna (LISA) aim to detect them, potentially revealing new insights into the universe's origin and the fundamental nature of gravity.

The study of gravitational waves also has profound implications for our understanding of fundamental physics. By testing the predictions of general relativity under extreme conditions, gravitational wave observations can help to identify any deviations from the theory, offering clues about the nature of gravity and its integration with quantum mechanics. Additionally, these observations may provide evidence for exotic objects like primordial black holes or boson stars, which are predicted by certain theories beyond the standard model of particle physics.

The field of gravitational wave astronomy is still in its infancy, with many discoveries yet to be made. As detectors become more sensitive and new observatories come online, the number of detectable events is expected to increase significantly, providing a wealth of data for scientists to analyze. This burgeoning field promises to deepen our understanding of the universe's most violent and mysterious phenomena, from the formation and evolution of black holes to the nature of dark matter and dark energy.

For beginners interested in the study of gravitational waves, there are numerous opportunities to engage with this exciting field. Many observatories and research institutions offer educational resources and outreach programs designed to introduce the public to the science of gravitational waves and their implications. Amateur astronomers and citizen scientists can also participate in data analysis projects, contributing to the detection and characterization of gravitational wave events.

The Expanding Universe Theory

The notion of an expanding universe is one of the most profound and transformative concepts in modern cosmology, reshaping our understanding of the cosmos and our place within it. This theory, which implies that the universe is not static but is continuously stretching, has far-reaching implications for the origin, evolution, and ultimate fate of everything that exists.

The seeds of the expanding universe theory were planted in the early 20th century, a time when the prevailing view was that the universe was eternal and unchanging. This perspective began to shift with the work of astronomer Edwin Hubble, who made a groundbreaking discovery while observing distant galaxies through the 100-inch Hooker Telescope at Mount Wilson Observatory. Hubble noticed that the light from these galaxies was redshifted, meaning that their spectral lines were shifted toward the red end of the spectrum. This redshift indicated that the galaxies were moving away from us, suggesting that the universe was expanding.

Hubble's observations were the first direct evidence of the expanding universe, but the theoretical framework supporting this idea had been laid a few years earlier by physicist Alexander Friedmann. Friedmann's solutions to Albert Einstein's equations of general relativity showed that an expanding universe was a natural outcome of the theory, even though Einstein himself initially resisted the idea. In fact, Einstein introduced a "cosmological constant" into his equations to maintain a static universe, a decision he later referred to as his "greatest blunder" after Hubble's findings corroborated Friedmann's expanding model.

The expanding universe theory gained further support with the discovery of cosmic microwave background radiation (CMB) in 1965 by Arno Penzias and Robert Wilson. This faint glow of microwave radiation, permeating all of space, is a relic of the early universe, a snapshot of the moment when light first traveled freely through space about 380,000 years after the Big Bang. The existence of the CMB provided compelling evidence for a universe that began as a hot, dense singularity and has been expanding ever since.

The expansion of the universe is often visualized with the analogy of a balloon being inflated. Imagine galaxies as dots on the surface of the balloon. As the balloon expands, the dots move farther apart. Importantly, the expansion occurs everywhere, not just from a central point, meaning every galaxy observes other galaxies moving away from it, giving the impression of being at the center of expansion. This realization underscores the concept of homogeneity and isotropy in cosmology, where the universe is roughly the same in all directions and locations on a large scale.

Hubble's Law quantifies the relationship between the distance of a galaxy and its recessional velocity, stating that the farther away a galaxy is, the faster it is moving away from us. This linear relationship is expressed as $v = H_0 \times d$, where v is the galaxy's velocity, H_0 is the Hubble constant, and d is the distance to the galaxy. The Hubble constant, a crucial parameter in cosmology, represents the rate of expansion and has been a subject of intense study and refinement over the decades.

The discovery of the universe's expansion led to the development of the Big Bang theory, the prevailing cosmological model describing the universe's birth and evolution. According to this theory, the universe began approximately 13.8 billion years ago from an extremely hot and dense state and has been expanding and cooling ever since. The Big Bang model explains a wide range of observations, from the abundance of light elements in the universe to the large-scale structure of galaxies and galaxy clusters.

An intriguing aspect of the expanding universe is the role of dark energy, a mysterious force driving the accelerated expansion of the universe. In the late 1990s, two independent teams of astronomers studying distant supernovae discovered that the universe's expansion is not slowing down, as previously expected, but is instead speeding up. This acceleration suggests the presence of dark energy, which is believed to make up about 68% of the universe's total energy content. While its exact nature remains elusive, dark energy is a key focus of contemporary cosmological research, with the potential to unlock new insights into the fundamental laws governing the universe.

The expanding universe theory raises profound questions about the ultimate fate of the cosmos. Several scenarios have been proposed, each with different implications for the future. The "Big Freeze" or "Heat Death" scenario posits that the universe will continue expanding indefinitely, leading to an eventual state where galaxies drift apart, stars burn out, and matter becomes uniformly distributed, resulting in a cold, dark, and lifeless universe. Alternatively, the "Big Rip" hypothesis suggests that the accelerated expansion driven by dark energy could eventually tear apart galaxies, stars, and even atomic structures, ending the universe in a catastrophic disintegration.

On a more optimistic note, some theories propose a cyclical model, where the universe undergoes repeated cycles of expansion and contraction. In this scenario, the universe might eventually collapse back into a hot, dense state, potentially leading to a new Big Bang and the birth of a new universe. However, this idea remains speculative and requires further theoretical and observational support.

Chapter 6: Myths and Legends Under the Stars

Ancient Stories of the Sky

Before the advent of modern science and technology, ancient civilizations looked to the sky, weaving stories that mirrored their beliefs, fears, and hopes. The night sky served as a canvas for storytelling, where constellations and celestial phenomena were depicted as divine narratives, guiding societies through the mysteries of existence. These ancient stories of the sky are not only fascinating tales but also reflections of cultural values and human imagination.

The Greeks, renowned for their mythology, populated the heavens with gods, heroes, and mythical creatures. The constellation Orion, for example, is named after the mighty hunter of Greek legend. Orion's story is one of hubris and tragedy. He was said to be the son of Poseidon, capable of walking on water, and was a formidable hunter. However, his boastful claim to kill every beast on Earth angered the goddess Gaia, who sent a scorpion to challenge him. This battle led to both Orion and the scorpion being immortalized in the sky as constellations, forever pursuing each other across the celestial sphere.

In Egyptian mythology, the sky was a realm of gods, with the Milky Way representing the celestial Nile. The ancient Egyptians believed the sun god Ra traveled across the sky each day in his solar barque, bringing light and life to the world. At night, Ra journeyed through the underworld, battling chaos and darkness before rising anew at dawn. The cyclical nature of this journey symbolized the eternal cycle of life, death, and rebirth, underscoring the Egyptians' reverence for cosmic order and continuity.

The Chinese sky mythology is rich with symbolism and celestial bureaucracy. The Jade Emperor, a central figure in Chinese mythology, presided over the heavens, earth, and the underworld. The Chinese zodiac, a twelve-year cycle represented by animals such as the Rat, Ox, and Dragon, was believed to influence personality traits and destiny. These celestial animals were said to participate in a great race organized by the Jade Emperor, determining their order in the zodiac and imbuing the sky with stories of cunning, strength, and perseverance.

In the Americas, the Native American tribes developed their own celestial narratives, often tying them to natural cycles and earthly events. The Lakota people, for instance, saw the stars as relatives and believed their ancestors dwelled in the sky. The Seven Sisters, known to Western astronomers as the Pleiades, were particularly significant. According to Lakota tradition, these stars were once seven beautiful maidens pursued by a bear. To escape, they climbed a high rock, which grew into the Black Hills, and they ascended into the sky, becoming a constellation. This story highlights themes of protection, transformation, and the sacredness of the land.

In Australia, Aboriginal cultures possess intricate sky lore, passed down through oral tradition for thousands of years. The Emu in the Sky, a dark constellation formed by the dust lanes of the Milky

Way, is a prominent feature in many Aboriginal stories. For the Yolngu people, the emu represents the spirit of a giant emu that once roamed the earth. Its appearance in the sky heralds the time for emu egg harvesting, illustrating how these stories are deeply interwoven with the natural world and survival.

As we move across the world, the Maya civilization also stands out for its sophisticated understanding of astronomy and its integration with their mythology. The Maya conceived the universe as a series of layers, with the sky serving as a bridge between the earthly realm and the divine. The movements of celestial bodies were meticulously recorded and interpreted as messages from the gods. Venus, in particular, was associated with the god Kukulkan and was believed to influence warfare and agriculture. The Maya constructed elaborate calendars and aligned their cities with astronomical events, reflecting their belief in the interconnectedness of cosmic and earthly affairs.

The Norse sky mythology, rooted in the harsh landscapes of Scandinavia, features gods and creatures battling for control of the heavens. The constellation Ursa Major was known as Odin's Wagon, representing the god Odin's chariot as he traversed the sky. The Northern Lights, or Aurora Borealis, were thought to be the reflections of Valkyries' armor as they escorted fallen warriors to Valhalla. These stories embody the Norse values of bravery, honor, and the eternal struggle between order and chaos.

These ancient stories of the sky not only provided explanations for celestial phenomena but also served as moral and ethical guides for the communities that told them. They offered a sense of connection to the cosmos, grounding human experience within a larger, divine narrative. Through the lens of mythology, the sky became a shared heritage, linking generations through a tapestry of stories that continue to inspire awe and wonder.

Celestial Deities and Their Tales

Throughout history, civilizations across the globe have gazed skyward, finding in the celestial sphere not only a source of wonder but also a pantheon of deities that captured the hearts and minds of their people. These celestial deities and their tales are woven into the fabric of cultural identity, embodying the mysteries of the heavens and the human quest to understand the universe.

In ancient Mesopotamia, one of the earliest cradles of civilization, the sky was a realm populated by powerful gods who governed the forces of nature and human fate. Anu, the supreme sky god, ruled over the heavens with an air of detached authority. His son, Enlil, wielded the power of the wind and storms, serving as a mediator between the divine and earthly realms. The goddess Inanna, associated with the planet Venus, was revered for her beauty and was celebrated in epic tales of love and war. These deities represented the unpredictable and often capricious nature of the elements, reflecting the precarious existence of the people who worshipped them.

The Egyptians, with their deep connection to the celestial and the eternal, revered a complex pantheon of sky gods and goddesses. One of the most prominent was Nut, the goddess of the sky, depicted as a star-covered woman arching over the earth. Her body formed the vault of the heavens, and each night, she swallowed the sun god Ra, giving birth to him anew each morning. This cycle of death and rebirth underscored the Egyptians' belief in the eternal cycle of life, mirrored in the constant motion of the stars and planets.

Ra himself was a central figure in Egyptian cosmology, embodying the sun's life-giving warmth and light. His daily journey across the sky in his solar barque was fraught with danger, particularly during his nightly passage through the underworld. There, he battled the serpent Apep, a symbol of chaos and darkness. Ra's triumph over Apep each dawn symbolized the victory of order over chaos, reinforcing the cosmic balance essential to Egyptian theology.

The Greeks, with their rich tradition of mythology, saw the sky as a tapestry of divine narratives, each constellation a story told by the gods. Zeus, the ruler of Mount Olympus, wielded thunderbolts from the heavens, his presence felt in every storm. His brother, Poseidon, was not only the god of the sea but also connected to earthquakes and horses, illustrating the interconnectedness of sky and earth in Greek thought. The goddess Artemis, protector of the wilderness and the moon, was often depicted as a huntress, her arrows shining as stars in the night sky.

One of the most enduring tales from Greek mythology is that of Phaethon, the son of Helios, the sun god. Desperate to prove his divine parentage, Phaethon convinced Helios to let him drive the sun chariot for a day. However, unable to control the powerful horses, he veered too close to the earth, scorching the land, before Zeus intervened with a thunderbolt, casting Phaethon into the river Eridanus. This tale serves as a cautionary reminder of the hubris and the dangers of overreaching, a theme reflected in the celestial order maintained by the gods.

In the Hindu tradition, the cosmos is a divine manifestation, with celestial deities embodying the fundamental forces of the universe. Surya, the sun god, is revered as the source of all life, riding his chariot across the sky, drawn by seven horses representing the colors of the rainbow. Chandra, the moon god, governs the night and influences the tides, embodying the cyclical nature of time and existence.

The Rigveda, one of the oldest sacred texts, describes the celestial deities Agni, the fire god, and Indra, the god of thunder and rain, as vital forces in the cosmic order. These deities are celebrated in hymns and rituals, reflecting the ancient belief in the interconnectedness of the divine and the natural world. Through their stories, the Vedic people sought to understand the rhythms of the universe and their place within it.

In the rich tapestry of Chinese mythology, the Jade Emperor reigns supreme over the celestial bureaucracy, overseeing the heavens, earth, and the underworld. The lunar goddess Chang'e, whose tale is celebrated during the Mid-Autumn Festival, is a symbol of immortality and beauty. According to legend, she consumed an elixir of life, ascending to the moon, where she resides with the Jade Rabbit, a companion who pounds the elixir under a cassia tree.

The story of the Weaver Girl and the Cowherd, immortalized in the stars as the constellations Vega and Altair, is a poignant tale of love and separation. Once a year, on the seventh day of the seventh lunar month, magpies form a bridge across the Milky Way, allowing the lovers to reunite. This tale speaks to the enduring power of love and the celestial forces that govern human destiny.

In the mythology of the Inca civilization, the sun god Inti was venerated as the progenitor of the Inca people, his warmth and light essential for agriculture and sustenance. The moon goddess Mama Quilla, wife of Inti, was associated with fertility and the passage of time. The Milky Way, known as Mayu, was seen as a celestial river, its meandering path reflecting the earthly rivers that sustained life in the harsh Andean environment.

The tales of celestial deities are as diverse as the cultures that tell them, yet they share common themes of creation, order, and the quest for understanding. These stories reflect humanity's enduring fascination with the sky and the desire to find meaning in the vastness of the universe. They remind us of the deep connection between the celestial and the terrestrial, a bond that has shaped human history and continues to inspire us today.

The Influence of Astrology

Astrology, the belief that celestial bodies influence human affairs and natural phenomena, has been a part of cultural traditions and personal belief systems for millennia. Despite the rise of modern science, astrology continues to captivate many, offering insights into personality, relationships, and life events. Its enduring appeal lies in its ability to provide a framework for understanding the complexities of human experience and the universe.

The roots of astrology trace back to ancient civilizations, where observing the night sky was both a practical and spiritual endeavor. The Babylonians, among the earliest practitioners, developed a sophisticated system of celestial divination around 2000 BCE. They divided the sky into twelve sections, each associated with a constellation, laying the groundwork for the zodiac as we know it today. This system was later adopted and refined by the Greeks, who infused it with their own mythology and philosophical ideas.

Astrology's influence spread across cultures, with each society adapting it to fit their worldview. In ancient Egypt, the stars were seen as manifestations of the gods, and astrology was intertwined with religion. The Egyptians believed that the positions of the stars and planets at the time of one's birth could reveal divine will and provide guidance for life. Similarly, in India, Vedic astrology, or Jyotisha, became a vital part of Hindu culture, influencing everything from daily activities to major life decisions.

During the Middle Ages, astrology was deeply integrated into European thought, with scholars and scientists alike studying its principles. Figures such as Johannes Kepler and Galileo Galilei, known for their contributions to astronomy, also dabbled in astrology, reflecting the blurred lines between science and mysticism at the time. Astrology was considered a legitimate discipline, influencing medical practices, political decisions, and personal choices.

The Renaissance era saw a resurgence of interest in astrology, as it became intertwined with the burgeoning field of astronomy. Astrologers were often consulted by rulers and nobles for advice on matters of state, marriage, and health. The belief in cosmic influence extended to the arts, with writers like William Shakespeare incorporating astrological themes into their works. This period marked a high point for astrology's influence, as it permeated various aspects of society.

In the modern era, astrology experienced both skepticism and revival. The Enlightenment, with its emphasis on reason and empirical evidence, led to a decline in astrology's scientific credibility. However, astrology found a new audience in the 20th century, particularly during the counterculture movements of the 1960s and 70s. Today, astrology enjoys a resurgence, thanks in part to digital media and the internet, which have made horoscopes and astrological content more accessible to a global audience.

The appeal of astrology lies in its ability to offer personal insights and a sense of connection to the cosmos. Many people turn to astrology as a tool for self-reflection, using their birth charts to explore personality traits, strengths, and challenges. A birth chart, or natal chart, is a map of the sky at the exact moment of one's birth, detailing the positions of the sun, moon, and planets. Each celestial body is believed to govern different aspects of life, providing a unique cosmic fingerprint for every individual.

Astrology also offers guidance in relationships, both personal and professional. By comparing the astrological charts of two individuals, astrologers claim to assess compatibility, identifying potential areas of harmony and conflict. This practice, known as synastry, has become popular in matchmaking and relationship counseling, offering a lens through which to understand interpersonal dynamics.

In addition to personal insights, astrology provides a framework for interpreting life events and cycles. The movement of planets through the zodiac is believed to influence global and individual experiences, with certain alignments heralding periods of growth, challenge, or change. Astrologers interpret these cosmic patterns to offer predictions and advice, helping individuals navigate the uncertainties of life.

While astrology's scientific validity remains a topic of debate, its psychological and cultural impact is undeniable. For many, astrology serves as a comforting narrative, providing meaning and order in a chaotic world. It encourages introspection and self-awareness, prompting individuals to reflect on their place in the universe and their relationships with others.

Astrology's influence extends beyond personal beliefs, permeating popular culture and media. Horoscopes, once confined to newspaper columns, now feature prominently in online platforms, apps, and social media. Celebrities and public figures openly discuss their astrological signs, further fueling public interest and acceptance. Astrology-themed merchandise, from clothing to home decor, reflects its integration into everyday life.

Despite its popularity, astrology faces criticism from skeptics who argue that it lacks empirical evidence and scientific rigor. Critics point to the Barnum effect, a psychological phenomenon where individuals see vague or general statements as highly accurate for themselves, as a reason for astrology's perceived accuracy. This skepticism underscores the ongoing tension between scientific inquiry and belief systems rooted in tradition and personal experience.

For beginners interested in exploring astrology, it's important to approach it with an open mind and a critical eye. Engaging with astrology can be a rewarding journey of self-discovery, offering new perspectives and insights. However, it's crucial to balance astrological interpretations with reason and personal judgment, recognizing its limitations and subjective nature.

Nighttime Rituals and Ceremonies

Throughout history, the mysterious allure of the night has captivated human beings, inspiring rituals and ceremonies that bridge the earthly and the celestial.

These nocturnal gatherings served as manifestations of cultural identity, spirituality, and communal bonding, providing a stage upon which humans could express their deepest fears, hopes, and connections to the cosmos.

In ancient times, nighttime provided an ideal backdrop for rituals imbued with a sense of mystery and reverence. The darkness, punctuated by the glow of the moon and stars, created an atmosphere of introspection and spiritual awakening. Many cultures embraced the night as a sacred time, when the veil between the physical and spiritual realms thinned, allowing for communion with deities, ancestors, and the forces of nature.

The Celts, known for their deep connection to the natural world, held elaborate ceremonies under the moonlight. Samhain, one of their most significant festivals, marked the end of the harvest and the onset of winter. Celebrated on the night of October 31st, it was believed that the spirits of the dead returned to the world of the living. Bonfires were lit to ward off malevolent spirits, and offerings of food and drink were left for the ancestors. This festival, a precursor to modern Halloween, was a time of reflection, honoring the cycle of life, death, and rebirth.

In ancient Greece, the Eleusinian Mysteries unfolded under the cloak of night, shrouded in secrecy and mysticism. These rituals, dedicated to Demeter and Persephone, attracted initiates from across the Hellenic world, who sought enlightenment and a deeper understanding of life's mysteries. The ceremonies involved processions, sacrifices, and dramatic reenactments, symbolizing the descent into the underworld and the promise of rebirth. Participants emerged transformed, having experienced a profound spiritual journey that reinforced their connection to the divine.

The indigenous peoples of North America also held sacred nighttime ceremonies, often centered around the cycles of the moon and the changing seasons. The Lakota Sioux, for example, conducted the Night Dance, a ceremony to honor the spirits of their ancestors and seek guidance for the coming year. Participants adorned themselves with ceremonial attire, danced around a central fire, and sang songs passed down through generations. These rituals reinforced communal bonds and emphasized the importance of harmony with the natural world.

In the dense rainforests of the Amazon, the indigenous tribes practiced shamanic rituals that harnessed the transformative power of the night. Ayahuasca ceremonies, led by experienced shamans, involved the ingestion of a potent plant brew that induced visions and spiritual revelations. Conducted in the darkness of night, these ceremonies were journeys into the soul, offering insight, healing, and a connection to the spirit world. Participants emerged with a renewed sense of purpose and understanding, their experiences woven into the rich tapestry of their cultural heritage.

The ancient Egyptians, whose civilization was deeply intertwined with the cycles of the heavens, held nighttime rituals dedicated to their pantheon of gods. The Opet Festival, celebrated during the inundation of the Nile, was a grand spectacle that included a nighttime procession of statues from Karnak to Luxor. The procession, illuminated by torches and accompanied by music and dance, symbolized the renewal of divine power and the fertility of the land. These ceremonies reinforced the Egyptians' belief in the cosmic order and the eternal connection between the gods and humanity.

In the Islamic world, the Night of Power, or Laylat al-Qadr, is observed during the last ten days of Ramadan. It is believed to be the night when the Quran was first revealed to the Prophet Muhammad, and it holds immense spiritual significance. Muslims engage in prayer, reflection, and recitation of the Quran, seeking forgiveness and spiritual elevation. The night is a time of profound connection with the divine, and its observance is considered to be more rewarding than a thousand months of worship.

In Japan, the Obon Festival is a time of remembrance and gratitude, celebrated with nighttime lantern ceremonies. Families gather to honor the spirits of their ancestors, lighting lanterns to guide them back to the world of the living. The festival culminates in the Toro Nagashi, where paper lanterns are set afloat on rivers, symbolically guiding spirits back to the afterlife. This beautiful and poignant ritual underscores the Japanese reverence for family, tradition, and the transient nature of life.

Modern society, with its ever-present artificial light and fast-paced lifestyle, often disconnects us from the profound experiences of night. However, contemporary movements have sought to revive and adapt nighttime rituals, reclaiming the night as a time for reflection, connection, and celebration. Full moon gatherings, stargazing parties, and urban retreats offer unique opportunities to reconnect with the natural world and explore the mysteries of the night.

For beginners interested in participating in or organizing nighttime rituals, it's important to approach these gatherings with respect, mindfulness, and an open heart. Consider the cultural context and significance of the rituals, and seek guidance from knowledgeable practitioners when possible. Whether it's a solitary meditation under the stars or a communal celebration, the night offers a canvas for exploration, transformation, and connection.

Modern Interpretations of Myths

The myths of ancient cultures have long served as a wellspring of wisdom and storytelling, their themes and archetypes resonating through the ages. As the world has evolved, so too have the interpretations of these timeless narratives. In the modern era, myths are reimagined and reinterpreted to reflect contemporary values, societal changes, and the complexities of the human experience. This dynamic interplay between ancient stories and modern sensibilities offers a rich tapestry of meaning, inviting us to explore the enduring relevance of myths in our lives.

One of the most captivating aspects of myths is their ability to adapt to changing times. Modern retellings often place traditional stories in new contexts, allowing them to address current issues and resonate with today's audiences. For example, the Greek myth of Icarus, who flew too close to the sun, is frequently used as a metaphor for the dangers of hubris and overambition. In contemporary interpretations, Icarus's story is often expanded to explore themes of parental pressure, the pursuit of personal dreams, and the consequences of ignoring cautionary advice. This reinterpretation prompts reflection on the balance between aspiration and recklessness in our own lives.

Similarly, the myth of Persephone, whose annual descent into the underworld heralds the changing seasons, has been reinterpreted to explore themes of empowerment and transformation. In modern retellings, Persephone is often portrayed not as a passive victim but as an active participant in her own story, making choices and asserting her agency. This shift reflects a broader cultural movement toward recognizing the strength and autonomy of women, resonating with contemporary conversations around gender equality and female empowerment.

The Norse myth of Ragnarok, the apocalyptic battle that brings about the end of the world, has found new life in modern narratives as a metaphor for environmental collapse and the urgent need for conservation. As climate change and ecological degradation become pressing global concerns, storytellers draw on the imagery of Ragnarok to highlight the interconnectedness of all living things and the consequences of humanity's actions. This reinterpretation serves as both a warning and a call to action, urging us to take responsibility for our planet and work toward a sustainable future.

In the realm of popular culture, myths are reimagined through various media, including literature, film, and television. These adaptations often blend elements of the original stories with contemporary genres, creating fresh and engaging narratives. The Marvel Cinematic Universe, for instance, draws heavily on Norse mythology, reimagining gods like Thor and Loki as superheroes with complex personalities and moral dilemmas. This fusion of myth and modern storytelling techniques allows ancient tales to reach new audiences, bridging the gap between the past and the present.

The reinterpretation of myths also extends to the exploration of identity and cultural heritage. Authors and creators from diverse backgrounds draw on their own mythological traditions to craft stories that reflect their unique experiences and perspectives. These narratives often challenge dominant cultural narratives, offering alternative viewpoints and enriching the tapestry of global storytelling. By weaving together ancient myths with contemporary themes, these creators celebrate the richness of their cultural heritage while addressing the complexities of modern life.

In addition to their narrative power, modern interpretations of myths often incorporate psychological insights, shedding light on the human psyche and our internal struggles. The work of psychologists like Carl Jung, who explored the concept of archetypes, has influenced the way we understand and engage with myths. Archetypes, such as the hero, the mentor, and the shadow, serve as universal symbols that resonate across cultures and time periods. By examining these archetypes within mythological narratives, we gain a deeper understanding of our own motivations, fears, and desires.

The hero's journey, a narrative pattern identified by Joseph Campbell, is a quintessential example of how myths continue to shape modern storytelling. This journey, characterized by the protagonist's departure, initiation, and return, serves as a framework for countless stories across different media. From epic fantasy novels to blockbuster films, the hero's journey remains a powerful tool for exploring personal growth, transformation, and the quest for meaning.

In the digital age, myths are also being reimagined and shared through online platforms and social media. Artists, writers, and creators utilize these tools to craft visual and textual interpretations of myths, engaging with audiences in new and innovative ways. This democratization of storytelling allows for a diverse range of voices and perspectives, enriching our collective understanding of these ancient tales. Through blogs, podcasts, and interactive experiences, myths are brought to life in ways that transcend traditional boundaries, inviting audiences to participate in the creative process.

* 9 7 9 8 3 3 0 5 5 5 5 6 7 *